GUIDE TO EMERGING MARKETS

OTHER ECONOMIST BOOKS

Guide to Analysing Companies
Guide to Business Modelling
Guide to Business Planning
Guide to Cash Management
Guide to Commodities
Guide to Decision Making
Guide to Economic Indicators
Guide to the European Union
Guide to Financial Management
Guide to Financial Markets
Guide to Hedge Funds
Guide to Investment Strategy
Guide to Management Ideas and Gurus
Guide to Managing Growth
Guide to Organisation Design
Guide to Project Management
Guide to Supply Chain Management
Numbers Guide
Style Guide

Book of Business Quotations
Book of Isms
Book of Obituaries
Brands and Branding
Business Consulting
Business Strategy
Buying Professional Services
Doing Business in China
Economics
Managing Talent
Managing Uncertainty
Marketing
Marketing for Growth
Megachange – the world in 2050
Modern Warfare, Intelligence and Deterrence
Organisation Culture
Successful Strategy Execution
The World of Business

Directors: an A–Z Guide
Economics: an A–Z Guide
Investment: an A–Z Guide
Negotiation: an A–Z Guide

Pocket World in Figures

GUIDE TO EMERGING MARKETS

The business outlook, opportunities and obstacles

Edited by

Aidan Manktelow

PublicAffairs
New York

Typeset in EcoType by MacGuru Ltd

info@macguru.org.uk

Library of Congress Control Number: 2013955894

ISBN 978-1-61039-387-4 (PB orig.)

ISBN 978-1-61039-388-1 (EB)

First Edition

10 9 8 7 6 5 4 3 2 1

Contents

Contributors and sources

Aidan Manktelow, director Europe, the Economist Corporate Network, edited the book. He also wrote the sections on economic megatrends, identifying market opportunities, governments and their policies, the manufacturing revolution, competition, rebalancing and transformation, management hubs, Russia, Poland, Turkey, Ukraine, South Korea and Algeria, and the emerging Europe overview.

Frida Wallin, formerly associate director, Asia, the Economist Corporate Network, edited parts of the book.

Rodrigo Aguilero, editor/economist, the Economist Intelligence Unit, wrote the sections on Chile and Mexico.

Vanessa Barchfield, formerly research editor, EMEA, the Economist Corporate Network, wrote the sections on talent management and ethics, and conducted interviews.

Federico Barriga, editor/economist, the Economist Intelligence Unit, wrote the sections on Colombia and Venezuela.

Edward Bell, editor/economist, the Economist Intelligence Unit, wrote the section on Iran.

Robin Bew, managing director and chief economist, the Economist Intelligence Unit, wrote the introduction.

Mary Boyd, director, Shanghai, the Economist Corporate Network, wrote the sections on China.

Toby Iles, regional editor/economist, Middle East and North Africa, the Economist Intelligence Unit, wrote the section on Iraq.

William Lee, editor/economist, the Economist Intelligence Unit, wrote the section on Peru.

Irene Mia, regional director, Latin America, the Economist Intelligence Unit, wrote the section on emerging-market cities and the Latin America overview.

Philip McCrum, editorial director, EMEA, the Economist Corporate Network, wrote the sections on Egypt and Saudi Arabia and wrote the Middle East and North Africa overview.

Ross O'Brien, director, Hong Kong, the Economist Corporate Network, wrote about competition, rebalancing and Indonesia.

Katharine Pulvermacher, director, Africa, the Economist Corporate Network, wrote the sections on corporate sustainability and responsibility (CSR), distribution, Kenya, Nigeria and South Africa.

Pamela Qiu, associate director, South-East Asia, the Economist Corporate Network, wrote the sections on Malaysia, the Philippines and Thailand.

Sujatha Santhanakrishnan, editor/economist, the Economist Intelligence Unit, wrote the sections on Bangladesh and Pakistan.

Pat Thaker, regional director, Africa, the Economist Intelligence Unit, wrote the Africa overview.

Robert Ward, country publishing director, the Economist Intelligence Unit, wrote the BRICs overview.

Justin Wood, director, South-East Asia, the Economist Corporate Network, wrote the sections on India and Vietnam and the Asia overview.

Robert Wood, senior editor/economist, the Economist Intelligence Unit, wrote the section on Brazil.

Coralie Zacchino, editor, Wire Services, the Economist Intelligence Unit, wrote the section on Argentina.

This book drew on research available in various parts of the Economist Group, including *The Economist* newspaper, the Economist Corporate Network, the Economist Intelligence Unit and Economist Education. Insights were also drawn from interviews conducted with senior business leaders operating in emerging markets, and from discussions with Delia Meth-Cohn, formerly editorial director, CEMEA, the Economist Corporate Network, and Lourdes Casanova, senior lecturer at Cornell University.

The Economist Corporate Network (www.corporatenetwork.com) is the Economist Group's business intelligence, briefing and networking service for senior executives of companies operating in emerging markets. It works closely with the CEOs and regional managers of over 400 companies such as Coca-Cola, IBM, DuPont and Dow Chemical.

Any comments about this book can be sent to Aidan Manktelow at: aidanmanktelow@economist.com

Introduction: the big shift and what it means for business

HONEYWELL INTERNATIONAL, a multinational conglomerate, has doubled the size of its non-US business in the past ten years, driven by growth in emerging markets. Shane Tedjarati, president, global high-growth regions, says that the company's business in China and India has been growing by over 20% annually since 2004. He points to the huge opportunities:

> There is massive urbanisation happening in high-growth markets, with very few exceptions. And these markets also require infrastructure. So there's huge spending on airports, seaports, on roads ...

There is also huge growth in consumer spending, which extends well beyond the largest cities and often involves very different levels of purchasing power compared with consumers in developed economies:

> The story of China is in tier two, three and four cities. It's in the mid-market, but a different mid-market than in the US. The Chinese mid-market is about $5,000 GDP per head.

Honeywell's success in emerging markets over that period came by radically changing its approach. Until 2004, it was basically a West-to-East company:

> One of our products could be slightly modified and sold in China ... But that model gets old very quickly. In 2004 we decided to take a fresh look at the market. We started by saying we were putting a lot more into understanding what the market is. So it was marketing,

R&D and putting a sales force together that really understood what kind of products our customers want, what features and at what cost. And doing that with local speed. Because these markets are fast ... and dynamic.

Manufacturing then followed.

The approach continues to develop and to lead to radical transformations in how Honeywell operates:

Our strategy, which we call East-for-East – design and innovate in China for China and in India for India – has now evolved and we've become East-to-West, because the products we're developing here will be needed elsewhere in the world. That strategy has worked very well.

This has required a major change of mentality, including empowering local operations. Tedjarati speaks of creating the spirit of an entrepreneurial Chinese company inside a large multinational company. Honeywell now expects "high-growth markets" to drive over 55% of its growth in the coming years.

Honeywell's experience reflects the rapid transformation under way in emerging markets. Companies cannot afford to ignore these countries, which will be the main source of global growth in the coming decades. But it also suggests that in order to succeed there Western multinationals will have to get used to doing business in different ways – and will fundamentally change themselves in the process.

Common characteristics

The very phrase "emerging markets" courts controversy. As a label, it lacks precision – being applied indiscriminately to countries which compete aggressively on the world stage, along with those trapped in subsistence agriculture or commodity extraction. More focused monikers, such as frontier markets (for those viewed as less developed and more challenging for business) and newly industrialising (for those bursting onto the global economic stage), may be more helpful.

Some companies, like Honeywell, are switching to growth markets or high-growth markets. But these terms are insufficiently nuanced as well – do growth markets always grow, and are companies really writing off growth in the developed world completely?

Emerging markets probably retain a greater hold among business leaders or commentators, so for the purposes of this book we acknowledge the difficulties but use the phrase anyway, as a means of describing collectively the markets of Asia, Latin America, eastern Europe, the Middle East and Africa which are of most interest to business leaders as current or prospective sources of opportunity.

In any case, some characteristics do bind this group of countries together. All have incomes per head substantially lower than the US, western Europe and Japan. All are less efficient – productivity is markedly lower than in the world's richest nations. But in these seemingly negative traits lies their promise. If inefficiency can be reduced, if workers can become more productive, if firms can climb up the value chain, then living standards can rise dramatically. The promise, alas, is not always realised. There are many examples of countries that are barely better off today than they were 20 or 30 years ago. Putting in place the right policies, setting up the right political and legal institutions and creating the conditions for growth, too often elude countries.

But where countries are able to see best practice and implement a version of it at home, the opportunity for business success beckons. Because rapid growth for these countries means overcoming major challenges – and in the challenges lie opportunities for companies. These are challenges of affordability, of meeting infrastructure needs, of coming up with new and innovative products to satisfy local tastes and customs. And there are the challenges of keeping up with rapid social and economic change. The CEO of a US automotive components supplier says that in China, where his firm supplies a large local manufacturer:

> The growth rates are just incredible ... The challenge of staying on top of the demand is certainly unlike any other country we have ever worked in.

Of course, even where countries get it right and experience rapid growth and rising living standards, the economic, political and business environments hardly match up to those in the advanced economies. Growth may be fast, but is often extraordinarily volatile, with regular crises knocking the country off course. Political systems are generally immature – corruption is often rife, bureaucrats are ineffective and policy decisions are driven by narrow special interests. And businesses often compete on a highly skewed playing field. For foreign firms hoping to profit from emerging markets, the opportunities resulting from rapid growth come with the complexities and risks of a challenging and sometimes capricious business environment. Rewards, as ever, are balanced by risks.

Historical rebalancing

The countries which are currently described as emerging were once dominant world powers. According to research by Angus Maddison, who was a professor of economics at the University of Groningen, China alone accounted for approximately 25% of the global economy from about 1500 until 1800, with India only slightly smaller. The US, now the largest economy in the world, was scarcely economically active at that time. But in the late 1700s Britain, followed by western Europe and then America, started to industrialise. The introduction of machinery, the use of steam power and the expansion of factories allowed productivity to improve. In the British textile sector, which industrialised earliest, the gains are estimated to have been a 20-fold improvement in output per person over the 100 years from 1700 to 1800, with some activities seeing even greater advances. Although the impact on the economy as a whole was smaller (since many other important sectors, such as agriculture, did not experience the same degree of mechanisation), this was sufficient to put western Europe and America on a growth trajectory which led to their domination of the global economy. Their technological lead meant that the gap in living standards between Western industrialisers and other nations widened dramatically.

Why did the emerging markets lag behind for so long? While it is a gross simplification to point to a single cause, many non-industrialised markets followed economic policies which cut them off from world markets and best practices (often not by choice – the impact of colonialism was also a major factor). Some used tariffs to keep imports out, in the hope that this would

FIG 1.1 **The cost of the crisis**

Difference, in % terms, of real output per head before the crisis started in 2007 and in 2012

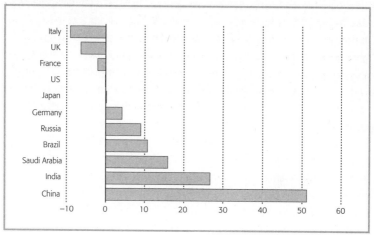

Source: The Economist Intelligence Unit

stimulate domestic industry to rise up and meet local demand. Often it did, but without the spur of competition such industries were weak and inefficient. Best practices from other countries – in everything from effective policymaking to institutional design, from application of the rule of law to corporate management techniques – were resolutely ignored as local leaders pursued narrow agendas often more concerned with retaining power than delivering growth. As a result, crucial infrastructure was not built and populations were left uneducated. Firms were not pitted against the best and therefore lacked the imperative to improve. Output per person languished and, as a result, countries remained poor.

Yet a 200-year period of Western dominance may be drawing to a close. Emerging markets are starting to narrow the gap with the West. Over the past 20 years, average growth in the emerging world has outstripped that of the developed markets by over three percentage points per year – even more at the height of the boom that preceded the 2008–09 crisis and while developed economies were laid low thereafter.

Catch-up between the emerging markets and the West has started because, one by one, countries have moved away from inward-looking strategies and begun to embrace global competition and adopt best practices. Perhaps the biggest and most well-known change of heart was in China, where Deng Xiaoping approved a series of economic reforms from 1978 onwards. The country was opened to foreign trade and investment, markets for products and services were opened to private businesses, some state-owned industries were privatised, and foreign technology and business practices were adopted. India followed suit with an economic liberalisation of its own in 1991. South-East Asia famously embraced foreign trade and became the region of both the Asian Tigers (South Korea, Hong Kong, Singapore and Taiwan) and other ASEAN growth stars such as Indonesia, Thailand and Malaysia. Latin America gradually liberalised too, with Brazil moving away from its policy of global economic disengagement in the late 1960s and Argentina reforming from the 1980s. In central and eastern Europe, reforms had to wait until the fall of the Soviet empire from 1989. In much of the former Soviet Union and Africa liberalising reforms remain patchy even to this day.

The pay-off from reform has been tremendous. In China, for example, income per head has risen from just 2% of US levels (measured using GDP per head at purchasing-power parity) in 1981 to 18% in 2012. The gap is expected to close further in the years ahead: by 2030 Chinese incomes will be running at about a third of US levels. Other countries have done even better – some of the Asian Tigers can truly be said to have emerged, with incomes per head approaching US levels. While not all emerging regions have benefited to the same extent, there has been a widespread acceleration in growth across much of the emerging world over the past decade, as governments have adopted more market-oriented policies.

Key trends

What of the future? Here are a few pointers of what to look for.

Catch-up will continue, but more slowly

It seems likely, although not inevitable, that many emerging markets will continue on the road of reform, and that incomes will rise more rapidly than in the West. But the pace of catch-up may still slow, in part because the global financial crisis has been such a drag on the advanced economies although it is reasonable to assume that they will recover at least some of their vim in the years ahead. Catch-up also becomes harder over time. Once the most effective policies and management techniques have been adopted in the emerging world, finding new ways to narrow the productivity gap becomes harder and growth therefore slower. And in countries such as China and Russia, demographic changes will further act as a drag on growth as their populations age. Nevertheless, even with a slower pace of catch-up, the emerging world will be where the growth is for business in the decades to come.

The biggest economies will not be the richest

China, India and other high-population countries are moving rapidly up the global economy league table. China is forecast to overtake the US by 2020. But China has five times as many people as the US, and its citizens will be considerably poorer on average than their Western counterparts. This means that companies will not just be able to farm out products developed with more affluent Western consumers in mind – pricing will be key.

FIG 1.2 **Collectively rich, individually poor**

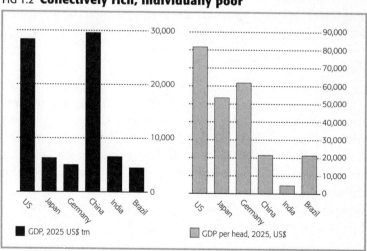

Source: The Economist Intelligence Unit

No convergence of politics

It was once fashionable to predict that, as emerging economies liberalised their business environment and became wealthier, they would also become more socially and politically liberal. While it is true that new-found wealth does seem to bring popular demands for social freedom, there is little evidence that emerging-world governments are keen to respond to this. Companies will therefore need to get used to a world in which the largest economies are run according to very different rules and norms from those in the West.

Increased turbulence

Emerging markets are, by definition, immature economies. Often they have immature politics too. Economic and political crises are common – few countries that have embarked on the road to catch-up have proceeded smoothly (think of the 1997 Asian crisis, the maxi-devaluations in Argentina, Brazil and Russia, and the uprisings of the Arab spring). As emerging markets become more dominant in the global economy, such crises will continue – even though emerging markets' resilience has increased and the 2008–09 crisis showed that Western countries are not immune from boom and bust either. But as emerging markets account for an ever greater share of global demand and spending, emerging-market crises will hurt more. So companies will need strategies that can contain volatility.

Reversals

Just because emerging markets have the potential to catch up with the rich world, this does not mean that they will. In many countries the basic ingredients necessary to allow productivity to rise are absent: economies remain highly regulated, or are run for the benefit of their leaders, or are socially fractious, or have non-economic priorities such as territorial or tribal ambitions. Some countries will not join the catch-up party. Others will leave the party halfway through. Companies will need to be able to identify those countries with the best chances of sustained growth.

Intensified competition

The competition for companies is increasing and changing. This is partly because any multinational will find that its global peers are also trying hard to increase their share in emerging markets. It is also because emerging-market companies are rapidly becoming much more serious competitors. They may enjoy advantages, including better cultural understanding, more appropriate business models, better relationships with government, entrenched protectionism and possibly fewer restrictions on how they do business. Some 20% of the Fortune Global 500 are already emerging-market companies – Chinese, Indian, Brazilian, Russian, South Korean and Turkish firms all feature. They will increasingly challenge Western firms not just in their home markets but globally.

Rich-world angst

This is a book about emerging markets. But Western attitudes towards the rise of the emerging world will be central to the way in which individuals and firms engage in the fast-growing countries. As the status and weight of the West decline, it is inevitable that worries will increase about a loss of influence, a loss of jobs, pressure on pay, increased demand for raw materials, the environment and the geostrategic intentions of the newly powerful countries. Business engagement in the emerging world will be complicated by rich-world angst about the global rebalancing.

Corporate rebalancing

Attitudes of Western businesses to emerging markets have also evolved. In the 1990s and to some extent in the past decade, the rise in business investment in emerging markets was driven by cost cutting and outsourcing, still primarily directed at catering for final demand in the developed world. But as consumption in the emerging world has surged, companies have come to see these as key markets in their own right. A 2010 report by the Economist Intelligence Unit (EIU) showed that three-quarters of companies surveyed see emerging markets as a source of new business growth. Only 23% were looking for a low-cost manufacturing base.

Indeed, the rise of emerging markets touches every sector. A list of major investment successes in Turkey by the country's investment agency includes big names across a range of industries: fast-moving consumer goods (Coca-Cola, Nestlé, Unilever), clothing (Mango), consumer electronics (Bosch, GE), engineering (Alstom, Schneider Electric, Siemens), automotive (Ford, Hyundai, Pirelli, Toyota), energy (Shell), chemicals (BASF), pharmaceuticals (Pfizer), agribusiness (Cargill), telecoms (Ericsson), IT (Intel, Microsoft), logistics (DHL) and finance (BNP Paribas, Citi, HSBC). Nor is the big shift just a story for FTSE 500 companies – medium-sized and even small companies are getting in on the act too.

The rise of emerging countries as markets in their own right has meant a shift in priorities. Many multinational companies initially tried to tap the demand in these countries by selling unadapted (and often substandard) Western products. But as emerging markets have become a more important part of global strategy, and as multinationals have faced growing competition in these markets both from their peers and from local firms, companies are coming to accept that emerging markets require dedicated products and innovations. Multinationals have also come to understand the need to become more local. This means not just establishing a local presence, increasingly staffed by local talent, but empowering it to take decisions so that local needs can be met and companies can keep pace with the rapid pace of change.

But these shifts still have a long way to go. Companies are hindered by the difficulty of grappling with the complexity of the emerging world, by resource constraints and by corporate rigidity. The changes required for success are far-reaching, requiring radical transformations in company organisation and even corporate culture. Ultimately, emerging countries need to become just as much home markets as the US, Japan or western Europe – companies need to become truly globalised.

In conclusion, the balance of the global economy is shifting. The process will be bumpy and potentially unsettling. But it is also inevitable, and therefore needs to be accommodated by anyone hoping to prosper in the new world order that will result, even if it requires companies to undertake major changes.

A guide to emerging markets

This book gives some pointers to how business leaders can cope with the changes, identify where the opportunities lie, manage and mitigate the inevitable risks, and compete successfully.

It is divided into two parts. Part 1 looks at the main opportunities and challenges. Chapter 1 examines the trends driving the growth of emerging markets and gives a view on how emerging markets will fare in the future. Chapter 2 looks at the extent to which emerging markets share similar characteristics in terms of business opportunities and highlights the role of market research in identifying where the opportunities lie. Subsequent chapters discuss the major challenges for business: dealing with governments and their policies; managing talent and the workforce; infrastructure and property; supply, distribution and marketing; innovation and research and development; ethics and competition; market entry; and corporate rebalancing and transformation.

Part 2 is a guide to the leading emerging markets. It starts with a chapter on the BRICs (Brazil, Russia, India and China). They may be old news, but they still account for a huge chunk of the emerging-markets growth story, offer vast untapped opportunities – especially beyond the main cities – and are crucial for companies looking to rebalance towards the emerging world. Subsequent sections cover the principal markets in emerging Asia, emerging Europe, the Middle East and North Africa, Africa and Latin America.

In general, the selection of countries is based on their size in terms of population, close to 30m or above, and GDP, over $100 billion in 2012. There are a couple of exceptions. Chile should not qualify in terms of population, but it is included because it completes the round-up of the "big seven" economies in Latin America. Kenya should not make it by size of economy, but as sub-Saharan Africa is currently a focus for many companies, including it provides more of a flavour of the opportunities there – and it is one of the leading markets attracting interest. The selection criteria mean that countries such as Ethiopia and Myanmar, which have large populations but whose poverty means their economies are still relatively small, do not make an appearance. Some of these countries will become important markets in time, and more adventurous companies are already expanding there.

Broadly, though, the countries selected are the ones that are likely to be of most interest to companies based on population and market size. This does not mean that they are necessarily bankers for growth. As the country sections make clear, some of them are considerably less attractive once dodgy business environments and questionable economic prospects are factored in. Including countries such as Venezuela and Iran does, though, have the advantage of giving a fuller picture of the diversity of the emerging world.

PART 1

Opportunities and challenges in emerging markets

1 The economic megatrends

THE SHIFT IN GLOBAL ECONOMIC GRAVITY towards emerging markets was already under way before the financial and economic crisis of 2008–09. The concept of the BRIC (Brazil, Russia, India, China) economies, introduced by Goldman Sachs, a multinational investment bank, in 2001, had gained widespread currency, and the Beijing Olympics in 2008 were seen by many as marking the entry of a newly powerful China onto the global stage.

The global crisis accelerated the change. In 2007, before the crisis struck, Goldman Sachs projected that China's economy would overtake that of the US in size by 2027 at market exchange rates. The EIU now forecasts that this will occur as soon as 2025, and in 2019 in purchasing-power parity (PPP) terms.

The speed of change is startling: the economies of emerging markets as a whole have doubled in nominal US dollar terms since 2005, compared with tiny growth in advanced economies. Emerging markets will generate over 60% of global growth in the next five years.

One reason for this is the effect of the crisis on developed economies. These will remain encumbered into the medium term by households' need to rebuild their balance sheets, banking-sector deleveraging that will constrain credit and sharply expanded public debt burdens. Another reason is that emerging-market economies have – with such notable exceptions as eastern Europe – demonstrated a new-found resilience. Growth either held up well during the 2008–09 crisis or returned quickly thereafter.

Emerging markets have not fully "decoupled" from advanced economies. Most still find it difficult to sustain high growth rates if crucial export markets in the developed world are struggling. But,

FIG 1.3 **The world's ten largest economies, 2000 and 2020**

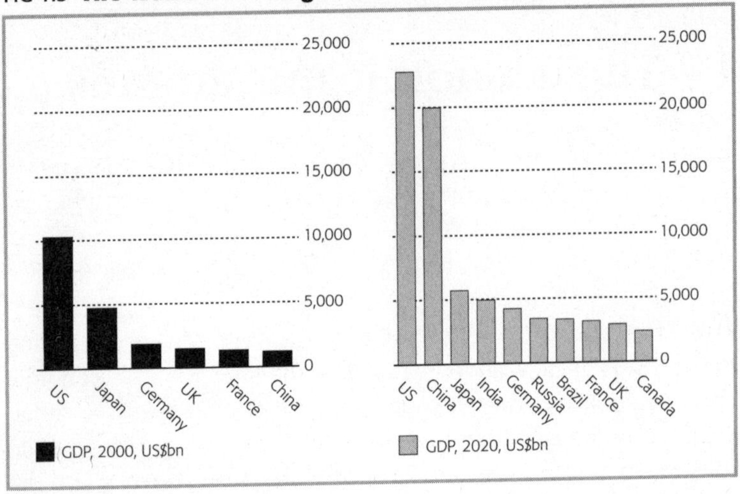
25,000
20,000
15,000
10,000
5,000
0
US
Japan
Germany
UK
France
China
GDP, 2000, US$bn
25,000
20,000
15,000
10,000
5,000
0
US
China
Japan
India
Germany
Russia
Brazil
France
UK
Canada
GDP, 2020, US$bn

Source: The Economist Intelligence Unit

unlike in the past, it appears that emerging economies now have sufficient internal drivers to grow robustly even while the developed world is in the doldrums.

Unfettered by developed-world solvency issues, many emerging markets are likely to continue to grow more strongly than developed countries in the coming years, allowing them to further narrow the gap with the developed world. Growth will be driven above all by increased openness, productivity catch-up, the improving quality of labour, the development of information and communications technology, and regulatory and institutional reform.

Rapid economic growth not guaranteed

The rise of emerging markets might seem unstoppable, but continued strong growth of these countries is not inevitable, and forecasts for the balance of the global economy in 2020, 2030 or even 2050 have to be seen as essentially hypothetical.

Emerging economies face a number of challenges. Their continued success will depend on their ability to improve productivity, which in turn will require institutional reform, which also poses political challenges. In countries that fail, growth will slow sharply once the easy gains of economic catch-up have been exhausted, and they will fall into a so-called middle-income trap of economic stagnation.

A key question is the future of China. The country has entered a new phase of its development, characterised by more balanced and slower output growth. It has already benefited from the productivity gains arising from the millions of peasants moving from farm to factory jobs, and future productivity gains will be harder to achieve. Its heavy reliance on investment to drive growth is also unsustainable.

There is also the real danger that economies in the West might respond to the rise of emerging powers by raising protectionist barriers. It is even possible that changes in the geopolitical order implied by the rise of the largest emerging powers will lead to armed conflict. And then there is the uncertain, poorly understood and often ignored impact that climate change may have on the global economy.

Developed economies will surely recover some of their spark in the longer term – there are already signs that the US economy is past the worst. Although prospects for western Europe and Japan look less promising, emerging markets will find it harder to narrow the gap in coming decades.

Moreover, not all emerging markets will succeed in making progress on catch up – some may fall further behind. For example, Venezuela's GDP per head in the 1950s was two-thirds that of the US; by 2012, following decades of economic mismanagement, it was one-quarter.

More complex picture

Overall, the outlook is more complex, and less certain than the "growth markets" tag might suggest. Growth rates vary across different markets including within the same sub-region. In central Europe, Poland's sizeable internal market helped it weather the 2008–09 global crisis. The more export-dependent Czech Republic struggled, while Hungary, which was undergoing a period of austerity following years of government overspending, fared particularly badly.

It is crucial to be able to pick out those emerging markets with the best chance of sustained growth. A decade ago, the BRIC markets concept provided a simple summary of the principal growth opportunities. Moreover, until 2008, most markets were being sustained by an expanding global economy. Life is more complex today. Companies have to grasp the full complexity of the emerging world, if they are to identify the growth opportunities and allocate their resources efficiently.

The next frontier: emerging-market cities

Throughout history cities have played a crucial role in generating prosperity, but today's unprecedented scale of urbanisation worldwide is heralding a major shift in economic power from state to city. Over 50% of the world's population now lives in cities, generating over 80% of global GDP. By 2050, 70% will be living in cities – compared with 1950, when 70% lived in rural areas.

The dynamism of emerging-market cities is particularly noteworthy. According to McKinsey, cities' GDP will increase by $30 trillion in 2010–25, of which 47% will be generated in 440 main emerging-market centres. The most dynamic will be in Asia, reflecting the region's recent economic rise, with 12 cities there expected to expand annually by over 10% in 2010–16 according to the EIU. This compares with annual growth of less than 4% for developed economies' cities, even in the most dynamic urban centres such as Dallas and Seattle. Cities in Latin America and Africa are also expected to grow rapidly in this period, with Lagos (6.8%), Lima (6.3%) and Bogotá (5.4%) leading the pack.

Reinforcing the emergence of cities as key economic actors is the dynamism second-tier, mid-sized cities (with populations between 2m and 5m) will display. In China alone, around 150 cities now have at least 1m inhabitants, and the number of cities is expected to increase to between 220 and 400 by 2020. While the EIU expects megalopolises to expand by an annual average of 6.3% in 2010–16, in second-tier cities the annual average growth rate will be just over 9%. So middle-sized cities will increasingly be the ones where the highest growth and best business opportunities are to be found. McKinsey estimates that the proportion of global growth accounted for by megalopolises will decline from over 70% to about 35% between 2012 and 2025, by which time almost 40% of growth will come from second-tier emerging-market cities.

Emerging-market cities will increasingly compete among themselves and with cities in the developed world for investment and talent, focusing on upgrading infrastructure and education as well as on making their regulatory environment as business-friendly as possible (including by providing direct and indirect incentives for businesses to relocate to their territory). Attracting the best talent in particular will be paramount. Developed-world cities have a competitive advantage in this respect, as indicated by the EIU's Global City Competitiveness Index, since, besides top-notch education and an abundance of high-end jobs, they offer safe environments with plenty of leisure activities. Nevertheless, emerging-market cities' dynamism and targeted policies are likely to start to redress the balance.

The expansion of emerging-market cities brings both opportunities and challenges for investors and businesses. The most obvious opportunities are no doubt in the sheer size of the consumer market which the growth of these cities will unlock, as well as their infrastructure needs. Urbanisation is normally accompanied by an increase in disposable household income: in China, for example, over the past 25 years, the per-head disposable income of urban households has increased five-and-a-half times in real terms, compared with three-and-a-half times for rural households. According to McKinsey, the ascent of cities in emerging markets will create 1 billion new consumers by 2025, giving a total of nearly 2 billion consumers located there. These cities will also generate over $20 trillion in consumption and investment in physical infrastructure.

City-focused strategies

To tap these opportunities, businesses will need to shift from country-focused to city-focused strategies, which entails important challenges. At present, few managers are taking their location decisions at city level and, according to a McKinsey survey, even fewer envisage changing their strategic approach in the next five years. Lack of awareness of the economic importance of little-known emerging-market second-tier cities can make businesses overlook their growth potential and miss important opportunities. Furthermore, planning at city level often requires a shift in mindset and organisational structures, which could be difficult to justify in a short-term view.

Last but not least, what is required for a successful city-focused strategy varies across industrial sectors and according to the target market. For some companies it would be enough to gain insight into general demographic and income trends; others would require more specific data on market dynamics for specific products in specific cities.

In sum, while the challenges for businesses are many, companies that prove capable of adapting to the new city-centric reality will find huge growth opportunities and new markets to conquer.

An opportunity for investors

Against this backdrop, concerns expressed by many commentators in 2013 that emerging markets were heading for a period of slower growth were arguably mainly a case of excessive expectations belatedly being adjusted. Still, even though it is likely to prove slower and patchier, the rise of emerging markets remains a historic opportunity for business. It is perfectly possible that over the next few years some 70% of the world's economic growth will come from emerging markets. Anil Gupta, Michael Dingham chair in strategy and entrepreneurship at the University of Maryland's Smith School of Business, argues:

> If we look at the next ten years, the rise of emerging economies will cause a bigger structural change in the world economy than any decade in the last 200 years.

Increasing private consumption, urbanisation and infrastructure development are important trends, presenting major opportunities in areas such as energy efficiency and food security.

Rising private consumption

■ Growth in the emerging countries will increasingly be driven by household spending, and especially by the expansion of the middle class. Private consumption accounts for roughly half of GDP in the BRIC economies. By contrast, in industrialised economies, the share is around 70%. So there is plenty of space for catch-up. China has already overtaken the US as the world's largest market for automotive sales; in Europe, Russia will overtake Germany in 2017, according to the EIU. A 2012 report by

McKinsey & Company, a consulting firm, forecast consumption in emerging markets to rise from $12 trillion in 2010 to $30 trillion in 2025, describing its projection as "the biggest growth opportunity in the history of capitalism". As these countries catch up, the nature of their spending will change. Households will devote less of their budgets to low-value-added goods such as food or furniture, and more to higher-value-added goods such as cars and household appliances.

Unprecedented urbanisation

- Emerging markets are now experiencing accelerated urbanisation – long primarily a developed-economy phenomenon – in the wake of industrialisation. Credit Suisse estimates that by 2037 emerging-market cities will account for half of the world's population, with the annual increase in their population peaking in 2035 at over 68m people, compared with 59m in 2012. Urbanisation will not just create new consumers, but also present huge challenges for governments in meeting the demand for infrastructure and services. Private operators may be able to help.

An infrastructure boom

- The world is currently witnessing the biggest infrastructure-investment boom in history – driven by emerging markets. Over half of the world's infrastructure investment is now taking place in emerging economies, where sales of excavators, for example, rose more than fivefold between 2000 and mid-2008. China spent more on infrastructure in the five years to 2008 than in the whole of the 20th century. India's 2008–12 five-year plan involved some $500 billion of infrastructure projects, and this is expected to double in 2013–17. Indeed, China and other emerging markets are investing more in infrastructure than today's rich economies did during their industrialisation. China has been spending about 12% of its GDP annually on infrastructure; even at the height of its railway mania in the 1840s, Britain invested only around 5% of its GDP in infrastructure.

2 Identifying market opportunities

THE OPPORTUNITIES ARE HUGE. But there are fundamental differences between developed and emerging economies from a business perspective. There are also vast variations across the emerging world and it is changing rapidly: the boundaries are blurring and differences are widening. Twenty years ago Poland could easily be seen in the same category as Ukraine; now it seems closer to Germany.

Some commentators argue that countries such as the BRICs should not be viewed as emerging markets at all; they have been firmly on the map for investment for over a decade.

But while this may be true for financial investment, it is less the case for the real economy. Emerging markets still have certain common characteristics from a business perspective, albeit to differing extents depending on the relative maturity of the market:

- Space for catch-up. Business growth can be expected to be faster than in developed economies as countries catch up from lower per-head income and market penetration levels (assuming a supportive policy environment). The pace of growth is slowing in the wealthier emerging markets such as South Korea, Chile, the Czech Republic and some other central and eastern European EU members, which are clearly approaching developed-economy status – but they are not completely there yet.

- Rising income levels. This means expansion of more wealthy segments, but also new categories of consumers and new business opportunities at the bottom of the pyramid. Emerging markets are both rich and poor at the same time. The emerging middle classes have growing disposable income but are poorer than their Western counterparts – China's per-head GDP approaching $10,000 (at PPP) compares with over $45,000 in the US.

■ Less consolidated market share. Market share is more fragmented than in developed economies and can change fast, so there is room for game-changers (although, again, less so in the more mature emerging countries). For example, Alibaba, a Chinese e-commerce company, was founded in 1998 and by 2012 had built up a business with annual revenue of over $4 billion (seeing off eBay in China in the process).

■ Risk and volatility. Risk and volatility is the other side of the opportunity and growth coin. It used to be assumed that potentially higher rewards in emerging markets were balanced by higher risks. But the balance has shifted – the rewards are now impossible to ignore, and the risks have diminished as governments have become more market friendly. Still, emerging markets remain more risky for companies than their developed-world counterparts in an operational sense, and even the macroeconomic risks remain considerable. The operational challenges are addressed in more detail in Chapter 3.

Top of the pyramid

It is essential for companies to understand the different income layers in emerging markets. Certainly, there are a growing number of consumers whose wealth, consumption habits and brand consciousness resemble that of consumers in companies' home markets. Many companies – notably luxury-goods companies – focus solely on serving this elite, and do not intend to move beyond it even as the wider market grows. They are merely skimming the surface of emerging markets rather than digging deep.

This can still result in strong growth. China has become a key market for Burberry, a UK luxury-goods group, accounting for 14% of its revenue – its sales in China rose by 20% in the year to the end of March 2013, for example. But although premium customers make up 10% of the market now, by 2025 the proportion will be only 3%. With the exception of luxury-goods companies, just focusing on premium segments where there are greater similarities across markets and trying to sell them Western products will not be enough to keep pace with the rise of emerging markets; companies need to be building a presence lower down, among the emerging middle classes.

Middle of the pyramid

The middle class in emerging markets is not a clearly defined demographic. It can encompass almost anyone with some disposable income, from the relatively affluent to those who still have to spend the bulk of their income on essentials. It may comprise anything from below 10% of the world's population to over half, depending on the estimate. What these people have in common is enough disposable income for regular spending on non-essentials. They can increasingly afford household appliances, cosmetics, computers, cars, and other such discretionary items – especially when rising incomes are allied to the ability to obtain credit.

While the overall size is open to debate, it is evident that the emerging middle class is expanding quickly. Surjit Bhalla, an Indian economist, has argued that the world is experiencing a third middle-class surge, following earlier instances in the 19th century and in the baby boom that followed the second world war – and this time the surge is taking place in emerging markets. McKinsey estimated in 2010 that by 2020, 900m people across Asia – more than the total population of the EU and the US combined – would enter the middle class, which it defines as $5,000 per head in PPP terms. This is enough to have a significant disposable income, but still mostly well below Western levels.

A crucial requirement for the middle of the pyramid in the emerging world is affordability. For example, General Motors sold 1.8m vehicles in China in 2009, but 1m of these were micro-vans and micro-trucks for use in farming, and the average price of these was just $5,000. The brands that are best able to take advantage of this shift will prosper. Nokia, a multinational communications and IT company, for example, managed to gain 60% of India's mobile phone market and 37% of China's – but only by developing cheaper products without compromising its brand.

But penetration of the middle-class market by Western firms is

FIG 1.4 **The expanding middle**
'000

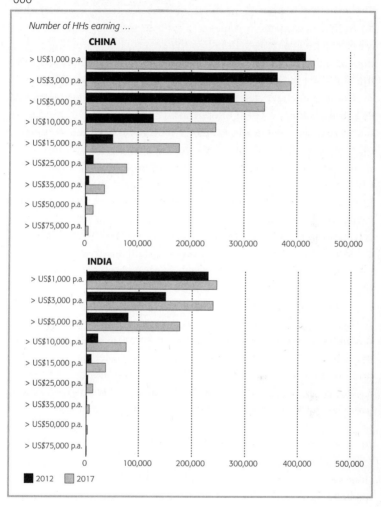

Source: The Economist Intelligence Unit

in general still relatively low. And as people's incomes are generally much lower than those of their Western counterparts, they typically cannot afford the same products. When IKEA entered China in 1998, many of its products were seen as upmarket rather than good value.

Bottom of the pyramid

The term "the bottom of the pyramid" was defined by C.K. Prahalad, an Indian management thinker, to refer to the people in emerging markets who live close to or below the poverty line, surviving on less than $2 a day. According the World Bank, around 2.5 billion people in the world are in this group – similar to the number in "middle class".

Companies have generally ignored this segment. But despite its lack of spending power, it offers considerable opportunities because of its size and unmet needs. And as economic development continues, many people will break out of this group and join the emerging middle class – in part because of continued urbanisation. For example, in China the government reportedly expects some 250m people to move from poor rural areas to cities between 2013 and 2025, which will lead to higher consumption even if many of these people remain poor. So companies (and marketing departments) looking for future volume are starting to think about how to build brand awareness among the poor and figuring out how to reach consumers in this group, even though the pay-off will not be immediate.

People at the bottom of the pyramid have to devote 60% or more of their spending to essentials such as food, fuel and clothing. They have little or no discretionary income or access to credit, so they are extremely price-conscious. These consumers are often paid by the day and buy their food at the local shop on their way home.

But people at the bottom of the pyramid still want good-quality products, so developing cheap, low-performance products for this segment is not the answer for companies. People will not aspire to them, and will shift to better products once they can afford to. Unilever found with shampoo that although poor people often wash their hair less frequently than wealthier people – as hot water is less available and affordable – they want to use a good product when they do. The solution is to offer a smaller packet of shampoo, which is cheap but still high-quality.

Prahalad argued that companies should not just be looking at income, but rather at how to create a capacity for people to consume:

This means that we have to change from a mentality of "my current costs plus profit equals the price" to a much more consumer-driven "price minus profit must equal cost".

Even if he overestimated how easy it would be to create good products at low prices, it is clear that companies would be unwise to ignore the bottom of the pyramid as a source of future growth.

Local differences

As well as the different income levels in emerging markets, companies need to understand local cultures and practices. Many reputable multinationals have tried to replicate their domestic models in emerging markets and failed because they did not realise that local differences would make them unviable. Things you take for granted in your home country may not exist. And lessons from one emerging market will not necessarily apply in another. "Each one is different," says the CEO of a US manufacturer of his company's experiences of setting up overseas. "Brazil is substantially different from Hungary, and China substantially different from Korea."

Customs and etiquette for doing business may be quite different, for example. In Brazil it is important to have clean nails, so Western managers would be well advised to get a manicure before visiting. In the former Soviet Union the need to do business over vodka has thankfully diminished – but it has not vanished yet.

Another example is family structures, which in many emerging markets differ considerably from those in Western countries. This has a major impact on the approach of consumer-goods companies. A company might need to know which consumer decisions are made by women and which by men; whether multiple family groups live in the same household; who takes care of children and the elderly; and whether there is significant sex discrimination. In India, where family is important and children value the advice of their parents, Pizza Hut adopted an advertising strategy that emphasised the Indian family's togetherness. Its early TV adverts featured the story of a couple in an arranged marriage meeting for the first time, and pizza breaking the ice.

It is also important to be aware that social norms in emerging markets are changing fast. For example, rising literacy and education rates and expanded job opportunities are giving women greater independence in many countries. A number of consumer-goods companies in India, such as Avon, have designed their marketing around the changing status of women in society.

Market research

With all these differences – between emerging economies and the developed world, and between emerging markets themselves – proper market analysis, research and planning are vital. Especially as other challenges, such as weak rule of law, political instability, currency volatility and infrastructure risks, need to be factored in as well. It is also important to anticipate moments when growth will leap. Demand typically follows an s-curve: rising strongly when a certain income point is met, which will clearly vary considerably depending on the product, and then tailing off once initial adoption is over.

Economic indicators are a key part of the equation but data in emerging markets are often incomplete or inaccurate – or non-existent. And it is important to go beyond the headline numbers.

Demographics

Commonly used demographic data include population growth, age, mobility, education and employment status. Demographics are an important determinant of a country's long-term economic prospects. Many emerging markets have young, growing populations, which can create economic dynamism and support growth in the years to come. But if jobs are not created for the young as they enter the labour market, there is a risk of countries squandering their demographic dividend and facing social unrest.

GDP

Gross domestic product (GDP) is one of the broadest indicators, helping to show an economy's size and the rate at which it is expanding. Nominal GDP includes price movements and so is a good measure of market size; real GDP strips out price effects and indicates how much the volume has changed. But many businesses are increasingly dissatisfied with GDP as an indicator of trends, finding it to be poorly correlated with the growth of their business. Trends in specific sectors may be detached from the overall growth of the economy, especially since the upheavals of the 2008-09 financial crisis, so GDP fails to provide an accurate measure.

It is important to beware of snap judgments based on a year or two of strong growth - countries' fortunes can change rapidly. In 2010, Brazil was flavour of the year as its economy surged to its strongest growth rate for decades at 7.5%. But by 2012 it became clear that its outperformance had been driven by loose monetary and fiscal conditions and growth slowed to around 1%, prompting more sober assessments of its potential.

And watch out for "base effects". If a country has recently suffered war, natural disaster or an economic slump, or undergone a big structural change, its GDP may well grow unusually rapidly for a period as it recovers. For example, Azerbaijan's economy grew by nearly 35% in 2006 and 25% in 2007 after a new oil field came on stream, but growth had fallen to just 5% by 2010.

Also be aware that unrecorded GDP may be high in emerging economies. All countries have "shadow economies" - black and/ or grey markets - but they are typically larger in emerging markets, where tax-collection systems are less sophisticated, perhaps up to 50% of GDP in some cases. A large shadow economy may mean that consumption is higher than suggested by official statistics.

Income

It is important to look at GDP growth per head as an indication of consumers' spending power. But go beyond the average, because income inequality is often high in emerging markets. In China and India, for example, average GDP per head is low, but this conceals the existence of 100m people with high incomes, whose consumption of luxury goods has been increasing fast. Distribution of income and numbers in each band are important.

Consumption depends not just on income and wealth, but also on interest rates, credit availability, expectations about prices and confidence about the future. If interest rates are high, people will find it hard to afford loans for big purchases. Deepening penetration of credit is supporting consumption growth in many emerging markets (but rapid rates of credit growth are not always sustainable, as eastern European countries discovered in 2008–09). If prices are volatile or the future is uncertain, people may spend more cautiously. Conversely, if the government subsidises utilities such as fuel or housing – not uncommon in emerging markets – private consumption may be higher than would be expected from per-head income levels. PepsiCo, a multinational food and beverage company, prefers to look at real disposable income.

Cultural and historical factors can also play a role. Russia's post-Soviet history of economic collapses and currency devaluations has made people more inclined to spend their money now rather than save it. Partly as a result of this, private consumption in Russia is 50% of GDP compared with just 37% in China. And if Russians are worried about an economic crisis causing a rouble slump or bank crash, sales of white goods rise, since people see them as a more reliable store of value.

Purchasing-power parity

GDP and GDP per head calculated according to purchasing-power parity (PPP) may be a better indication of what consumers in a country can actually afford than market exchange rates. PPP is calculated by comparing the cost of a basket of identical traded goods and services between two countries. The rationale is that locally produced goods and services may be cheaper than the equivalent abroad, so purchasing power will be higher than is implied by GDP at market exchange rates. The differences can be large. At the official exchange rate, GDP per head in India was around $1,500 in 2012. On a PPP basis, it was nearly three times higher. PPP is, though, a rough and imperfect calculation.

Inflation

Inflation is the rise of prices across the board. It usually refers to consumer prices but can also be applied to other prices (for example, producer prices and wages). Companies are generally fairly comfortable with a low level of inflation – low single digits. But once inflation approaches double digits – not uncommon in emerging markets – it becomes harder to budget and to plan long term. High inflation also squeezes spending power and discourages investment and savings.

Exchange rate

According to McKinsey, currency or exchange-rate volatility is the biggest concern for companies in emerging markets after intellectual property theft. Where supply chains straddle different currencies, or a company operating abroad measures revenues in its home currency, fluctuations can be disruptive. They can make costs soar, turn profits to losses and undermine otherwise viable projects. Attempts by countries to keep their currency from moving too much may also affect foreign companies, if this results in controls on capital flows.

But beware of using the nominal exchange rate as a measure of competitiveness. The real exchange rate also takes account of how fast prices are rising within a country. China's went up nearly 50% between 2005 and 2010, according to *The Economist*, which means that complaints about the country keeping the yuan artificially low to boost competitiveness were often overstated.

Proxy indicators

Indirect measures that approximate an aspect of the economy are often useful if headline economic data are patchy or unreliable. For example, under its eccentric dictator, Saparmurat Niyazov, Turkmenistan regularly claimed double-digit rates of GDP growth annually. But the amount of electricity consumed per head was rising in low single digits each year, suggesting the claims were questionable.

Due diligence

Properly evaluated, the opportunities in emerging markets are enticing, but thorough and realistic planning is vital. As the CEO of a US manufacturer moving into China and Brazil says:

Probably the longest part was our preliminary investigations – us learning more about the country, the culture, the geography, where our customers would be, where competition might be, the quality of competition.

Understanding the vast array of operating obstacles, and how to overcome them, is as important as identifying the opportunities. One of the greatest obstacles is government – its ideology, its policies and its general competence. This will be discussed in the next chapter.

3 Governments and their policies

IN 2010 VIKTOR YANUKOVYCH won the Ukrainian presidential election, beating the heroine of Ukraine's 2004 "Orange Revolution", Yulia Tymoshenko. Yanukovych, a convicted criminal, was backed by shady East Ukrainian business groups and there were questions about his commitment to democracy. Nevertheless, many foreign businesses welcomed the change. The "Orange" government had descended into messy political infighting and policy gridlock. The Yanukovych administration talked the talk on economic reform and European integration, and had an ambitious modernisation agenda. Businesses expected that improved political stability under Yanukovych would allow more progress.

Within little more than a year, the hopes had turned sour. Yanukovych was presiding over a roll-back of Ukraine's democracy, and Tymoshenko was imprisoned on charges that appeared politically motivated. Despite some modest progress, in general Yanukovych's oligarchic backers were more concerned with dividing the spoils than undertaking reforms; privatisations favoured the government's cronies. Foreign companies experienced worsening corruption, a sharp increase in visits from the tax authorities and arbitrary fines. Most put their plans to expand in Ukraine on hold and waited for things to improve.

The politics of an emerging market is crucial, both for its economic prospects and for the ability of foreign businesses to operate there. Problems that businesses face in connection with political turmoil or institutional weakness can range from revolution to more day-to-day issues such as inadequate legislation or corruption.

Political conditions in emerging countries vary widely. Many have made considerable progress in the past couple of decades in improving their institutions and implementing more business-friendly policies. But the challenges and risks for companies are still mostly higher – often considerably so – than in advanced democracies.

Political stability

Mature democracies are usually more prosperous and more stable than other forms of government, and have institutions that are more favourable for doing business. Countries may enjoy periods of rapid economic growth under authoritarian or semi-authoritarian regimes – as in China in the past couple of decades – but history suggests that without political change towards more inclusive institutions they will struggle to reach the levels of prosperity enjoyed by advanced economies. An important consideration for companies looking at a long-term presence in an emerging market is whether political inclusiveness and the quality of institutions are such as to support long-term economic catch-up.

However, multinationals often feel comfortable with autocratic rulers because they think they will ensure stability and perhaps be more effective at pushing through economic reforms. Certainly, in emerging markets new democracies can be volatile, or can become tied up in fractious politics. But as the upheavals in the Middle East during the 2011 Arab spring demonstrated, the stability of autocracies is brittle.

Furthermore, regime change, or even just struggles within the political elite, can seriously affect foreign businesses that are perceived to be tied to one side or another. In Russia, rivalries between government factions led to trouble for BP, a multinational oil and gas company, which had miscalculated the political cover that its ties to one group would provide.

Government effectiveness

But even where the rules of the game are stable, they can be difficult to live with. There is the question of whether the country's politics allows businesses to operate effectively. Governments in emerging markets are typically more intrusive and less transparent than their developed-world counterparts. Many institutions that Western companies take for granted are corrupt, badly run or simply missing. Governments and the judiciary can be incompetent or in the grip of vested interests. As well as making life difficult for business, this can put the country's growth prospects in doubt.

The extent to which a company will face problems may depend crucially on what its business is. In China, for example, negative stories include that of Rio Tinto, a multinational metals and mining company, in 2009–10. Four of the company's employees in China were arrested on charges of bribery and espionage. This happened during difficult negotiations between Rio Tinto and Chinese firms over the price of iron ore for 2009–10, and shortly after Rio Tinto refused to sell an additional stake in the company to China's state-owned Chinalco. By contrast, many Western companies enjoy good relations with the Chinese government. For example, Goodyear, a tyre and rubber company, won three awards from Chinese local governments in 2010 for credit performance and corporate social responsibility.

Generally, if a company is extracting a country's natural resources, or its activities threaten dominant local businesses, or its entry and growth are reducing state control over a strategic sector or society more broadly, life is likely to be more difficult. It is especially hard to compete with state businesses on their home turf because in effect they write the rules.

But in any sector it is possible that a government may move against a foreign business to help a local one, or to bolster support for its candidate in an election. Local politics can affect a company in unexpected ways. The US boss of a firm in China told *The Economist* that he was frequently denied permission to hold meetings for his sales staff, because the government feared that the outlawed Falun Gong sect might use them as cover for secret gatherings.

It is also possible that politicians – especially those inexperienced in how free markets work – might overreact if a business causes sudden changes. For example, in 2010 in the Indian state of Andhra Pradesh, a boom in microcredit led to many farmers being heavily in debt, and several committed suicide. This initially prompted the state government to instruct people not to repay their loans, which could have shattered the microcredit industry, until India's central bank intervened with more sensible guidelines.

Political culture

Companies need to make sure that they understand a country's political culture and the detailed political tendencies within the new market. What they need to know will vary from country to country: in China, it is the power dynamics of the Communist Party; in Brazil, Congress's multi-party alliances; in Russia, the business connections of groups within government; in South Africa, the residual influence of decades of apartheid. Overall, it is especially important to know who wields influence and how. Below are some crucial points to consider:

- What is the structure of political institutions?
- Are these institutions stable enough to support our needs?
- What is the government's attitude towards foreign direct investment, trade and business?
- How closely intertwined are domestic business interests with political power?
- How effective is the government at implementing policies?
- When are the next elections (assuming there are elections) and who is likely to win?
- How likely is it that an opposition party with a different agenda will come to power?
- How much autonomy from national government do regional or local leaders enjoy – in theory and in practice?
- What is the risk of social unrest? A young population and high unemployment could mean that trouble is brewing.
- What is the risk of international disputes?

One thing companies can consider when entering a market for the first time is whether any other businesses from their country and industry have succeeded there. What can be learnt from them?

Risk mitigation

To reduce the risk of government interference harming their business, companies should:

- Assess the impact of their investment on the economy. Promising to create jobs helps to get politicians onside. Posco, a South Korean steelmaker, won a favourable tax holiday in Indonesia as part of its $6 billion deal to enter the country in 2010, in part by pledging to create up to 200,000 jobs.

- Commit to building a business for the long term. An attitude of partnership and commitment is essential. Procter & Gamble took three years to become profitable in China. L'Oréal took nine. And KFC, which spent ten years perfecting its business model, now has restaurants in over 700 Chinese cities.

- Spend time developing political connections. Stanley Wong, head of Standard Chartered Bank's Chinese operations, says that senior representatives of multinationals in China must spend 30-40% of their time building relationships with officials and regulators.

The legal and regulatory climate

In late 2010 the Mumbai High Court ruled in a legal battle between Vodafone, a multinational telecommunications company, and the Indian tax authorities that Vodafone had to pay over $2 billion in capital gains tax relating to its acquisition of Hutchison Essar, a domestic mobile phone operator, three years before. This was the first time an Indian court had ruled that the country's tax department could charge a foreign company over a transaction outside India. Both companies were based in the Cayman Islands, so Vodafone had been confident that its transaction was not taxable in India. Indeed, it eventually got the ruling overturned by the Supreme Court. But this example shows that in emerging markets regulation is often uncertain and leaves scope for interpretation.

Thus it is crucial to identify all the possible obstacles, as these will have a huge impact on the success or failure of a business in an emerging market. Amit Sharma, executive vice-president at

American Tower, an owner and operator of wireless and broadcast communications sites, says:

> For most market entrants, the first five or ten years are largely driven by the regulations that govern them and only then do you reach the point where it's purely free market competition.

Issues to consider include:

- the vulnerability of the legal process to interference or distortion;
- the risk that contract rights will not be enforced;
- the speed and efficiency of judicial process;
- the extent to which domestic interests are likely to be favoured;
- the danger of expropriation;
- competition policy;
- protection of intellectual property;
- the reliability of business financial statements;
- price controls and the risk that these could be extended in times of economic stress;
- the tax code;
- investment incentives;
- possible obstacles such as local sourcing requirements.

Companies need to get as much high-quality advice as they can afford before market entry, and then keep up-to-date with developments in these areas afterwards. Tax, management, legal or political-risk consultants who know the market intimately will be able to help.

The tax system

Tax systems vary widely, but analysis by Pöyry, a global consulting and engineering firm, suggests some broad global trends:

- Nearly all tax systems have a corporate tax on net profits, typically around 30%.
- Extractive industries typically face royalties on their production.

- Firms in most countries face some form of profit-sharing tax, over and above corporate tax. In weaker tax systems this will often be on gross revenues.

Since the bulk of taxes are paid only on profits, most firms are concerned less about the marginal tax rate, and more about knowing which taxes they are likely to have to pay. This is where emerging markets differ most from developed ones: there is typically a much greater risk of unexpected tax reforms and surprises.

Some regimes decide to tax rich multinationals when their coffers run dry, or when greed overwhelms them. In 2006 the government of Chad suddenly demanded that Chevron, a multinational energy corporation, and Petronas, a Malaysian oil and gas company, pay $500m in taxes and give the government a share in their consortium. This was even though both companies had fully met their tax obligations under an agreement signed in 2000. The alternative was immediate expulsion.

Important points in assessing potential tax liabilities include the following:

- How stable is the country's tax regime? Do the authorities change the tax code frequently or unexpectedly?
- How sophisticated is the tax system? Inconsistencies can make liabilities unpredictable and create opportunities for officials to demand bribes.
- How favourable is the headline rate? In Estonia and in the Gulf countries, for example, taxes are low or zero.
- What taxes will be required in addition to corporate income tax?
- What concessions or exemptions, such as a tax holiday, might be negotiated in exchange for the company's investment?
- How long is it likely to be before the company becomes profitable and has to pay tax?
- How easy is it to repatriate post-tax profits? And how can it be done most cheaply?

Professional advice from an advisory firm with deep experience of the local market is essential.

Investment incentives and SEZs

Governments in emerging markets are often eager to attract foreign investors, and so may offer tax breaks, low import tariffs, express customs clearance, subsidised land or cheap power. They might have set up economic free zones or special economic zones (SEZs), with lower tax rates and simplified or suspended regulations, with the aim of encouraging a particular industry. China has been a leading exponent of SEZs. For instance, Shenzhen, north of Hong Kong, was declared an SEZ in the 1970s. At that time it was a small village; today it is one of the world's fastest growing cities, with a population of 10m.

Such zones may of course have costs, usually for the host country or local community. Lighter rules often lead to a bigger environmental impact, and in the case of labour rules, lower working standards are often allowed or ignored.

Local sourcing requirements

The World Trade Organisation, which most countries have joined, prohibits "local sourcing requirements" – rules that oblige companies to use locally made goods in their products. But governments often in effect force companies to source locally anyway, for example through tariffs on imported components. Local components may be cheaper anyway.

But when looking at the cost and availability of inputs – labour, raw materials, manufactured goods or technologies – it is important to identify anything that has to be imported and make sure that this can be done at a reasonable cost for the foreseeable future. For instance, a large part of the world's denim production is undertaken in Xintang, in China, but this is reliant on cotton imports from Pakistan, Australia, India and elsewhere. When floods devastated Pakistan's cotton crops in 2010, production costs for the denim factories in Xintang soared.

Trade quotas

Wherever businesses depend to a significant extent on imports or exports, they will be vulnerable to trade quotas, subsidies and tariffs, which are used by governments to protect domestic interests. For example, until 2009 some 80% of Australian beef was exported to Indonesia. But the Indonesian government wanted the country to become more self-sufficient and to protect domestic agriculture, so it reduced the number of permits for Australian beef importers, setting an import quota of 500,000 head of cattle for 2011. Australian beef exports dropped by almost one-third, and many Australian beef farmers faced difficulties (meanwhile the price of beef in Indonesia shot up).

Countries sometimes impose quotas or trade bans for political reasons. Russia is notorious for this. In 2006, for example, it slapped bans on imports of Georgian and Moldovan wines, for which it was the biggest export market, after falling out with the governments of those countries.

Quality-certification procedures

Quality-certification procedures can be used as a barrier to protect local industry. Most multinational companies have high quality-control standards, so emerging markets should in theory present no problem in this respect. But even though rules on the classification, labelling and testing of products might officially reflect health-and-safety concerns, in reality they may be designed to shut out products manufactured in another country. Overall, companies should carefully plan their import and export requirements against the trade conditions of the target country, and have alternatives if conditions change.

4 Managing talent and the workforce

MANY OPERATIONAL ASPECTS of doing business in emerging markets differ from country to country, but one issue heads management agendas around the world: talent. With their counterparts in global headquarters often focused on controlling staff costs and keeping operations in mature markets as lean as possible, managers in São Paulo, Moscow, Johannesburg or Shanghai have the task of recruiting, hiring, training and retaining talent in markets where the best and the brightest are fiercely sought after. This chapter examines how companies' approaches to staffing in emerging markets are changing, and highlights some best practices for recruitment, retention and good industrial relations.

The Western expatriate

For many years, companies' business in emerging markets was handled by expatriates dispatched for a few years from global headquarters. Managers who were sent abroad could expect a comfortable package: company car, centrally located apartment, membership of an exclusive country club and, of course, tuition for their children at an international school.

What such managers did not necessarily provide in return (at least to start with) was an intimate knowledge of the country they were sent to. Anil Gupta of the University of Maryland's Smith School of Business explains:

> *Fifteen years ago ... companies targeted the top 5% of the population. They used emerging markets to offshore their manufacturing. They had very little interaction with the economy as a whole. Expats*

worked just fine for this level of engagement. But today companies want to reach a large share of the middle or even bottom of the economy ... to do so they need a lot more senior managers – and there aren't enough expats to fill those roles.

But the diminishing role of the expat is not just a function of supply and demand. Even before the global financial crisis of 2008–09 propelled emerging economies to the top of corporate strategies, a handful of companies had recognised the limitations of having Americans or Brits, who may not speak Portuguese or Mandarin, running their business in Brazil or China. There has been a trend for several years for successful companies in emerging markets to try to substitute expats with local managers as soon as possible; and that trend is accelerating.

With international companies competing for market share – and contending with ever-stronger local competitors – the need for staff with strong connections, local knowledge and deep cultural understanding is more acute than ever.

So is the expat a relic of the past? Not exactly. The expat will remain crucial for businesses in developing countries across the Gulf and sub-Saharan Africa for some time because of shortages of highly trained professionals there. In the United Arab Emirates, Emiratis account for just one-eighth of the population, and there is a paucity of institutions of higher learning in sub-Saharan Africa (outside South Africa).

But forward-thinking companies are already planning the eventual phasing out of their Western expats in these markets as well, building partnerships with universities and creating training schemes to develop the soft skills that international companies require.

Localising talent

As the role of expats declines, the vacuum they leave will be filled with managers who are actually from – or at least have ties to – the local market. The challenge is finding the skills that international companies require in markets where educational systems have long emphasised rote learning (as in India and much of the Middle East), where soft skills go untaught (as in China), or where English skills are lacking (as in Brazil). So how are companies bridging the gap between skills that they need and those that are available in the local labour market? Some best practices are as follows.

Forge partnerships with universities

Many companies are working closely with universities to shape curricula and develop skills that are largely absent in many of their growth markets. One large industrial company conducts scientific research in collaboration with Saudi Arabia's King Abdullah University of Science and Technology, for example. A manager at the company believes that the partnership will help build a qualified pool of young Saudi engineers. "We're ramping up these sorts of programmes with universities in the region now," he said. Indeed, many managers say academic partnerships are high on the corporate radar. Not only do these partnerships develop skills that companies need, they also give firms their pick of the top graduates, notes Gupta. Another positive trend is the burgeoning of international MBA programmes across emerging markets.

Recruit outside the box

Most multinationals want specific boxes ticked when recruiting: leadership skills, self-reliance and most importantly fluency in English, as well as proven excellence in, say, engineering or sales. But this rigid formula for recruitment vastly limits the talent pool and, worse, perpetuates a vicious cycle of social exclusion, says Alfredo Behrens, Professor of Cross-cultural Leadership at the FIA business school in São Paulo. "International companies make English a prerequisite when hiring in Brazil. This restricts the talent pool to the privileged white elite," he explains. If companies removed the English requirement and hired people from less privileged backgrounds, they would get highly talented people they would not have considered before, people with more "grit", Behrens says. "And those people will become icons for others to follow."

Only once their new, more representative staff members are on board should firms concentrate on teaching English, and developing any other skills that their new recruits are lacking.

Sell the brand

While broadening the potential talent pool is one way of improving human capital in emerging markets, it is also crucial to "sell" the company to locals. "Employer branding is crucial," one manager said. "You need to start at a young age getting people interested in working for your company."

Another senior manager put it this way:

To draw the best talent available you really have to position your company as a good place to work. You need to stress the opportunities for career development – sell the idea that even an entry-level position in your organisation offers a chance to really develop. You're not just offering a job – you're offering a career.

Retaining high performers

One major concern across emerging markets is keeping high performers even when they are bombarded with attractive offers from the competition, both international and local. A senior manager at an international firm in the telecoms industry says his company has an attrition rate in excess of 25% annually in China, and similar turnover numbers in India. Some of the best strategies for improving retention in the red-hot labour markets across high-growth economies are as follows.

Career development

The promise of career development is not just a powerful recruiting tool; it is also one of the most effective hooks for keeping high performers. Many senior managers agree that transparency about how to ascend the corporate ladder is an even stronger enticement than higher salaries and other non-financial perks.

Work with high performers to set goals and establish clear benchmarks on how to achieve them; assign them mentors outside their chain of command in order to strengthen ties to the broader organisation; and of course, invest in training.

Another crucial element of career development, says one manager, is the existence of role models. "Asianise [or localise] management.

Demonstrate that there is clear room to move up in your company."

The big picture

Showing staff the big picture is another potent tool for retention. A major industrial firm registered high turnover in one engineering section of its operations in India. When management looked closely at the problem, they found that engineers who were working on one single component did not know what the finished product was at the end of the assembly line. This sense of detachment led to a constant stream of departures. One senior manager says:

> *Involve staff in the whole venture. If your staff are treated like pawns of headquarters, you won't be able to keep them.*

Foreign exchange

One difficulty in localising the payroll is aligning local hires with the global corporate culture. The most effective remedy is to post locally hired high performers to operations outside their home country. A senior manager at a large industrial firm says:

> *In order to understand the company, staff have to move around. We encourage rotation – taking expertise and sending it to operations outside their home base. This is helping us to become a truly global company.*

Rotating young high performers not only strengthens their ties to the company, but the experience will also broaden their worldview. Behrens says:

> *People in Brazil lack a global mindset, which can be a problem for international companies. That's hard to develop when people are in their 50s, but not when they're in their 20s or 30s. It might not seem justifiable to send such young staff members abroad, but this is the best way to build future leaders.*

FIG 1.5 **Labour costs per hour**
US$, average

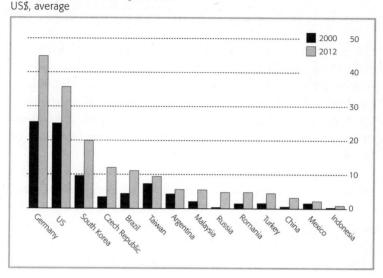

Source: The Economist Intelligence Unit

Labour costs

As well as talent management, there are other workforce challenges facing companies in emerging markets. Rapid changes in labour costs is one.

Although the days of multinational companies looking at emerging markets purely as locations for low-cost manufacturing are long gone, lower labour costs are still an important consideration for many companies. As Figure 1.5 shows, there are huge variations in average staff costs in emerging economies.

Wages are rising rapidly in many markets, reflecting high rates of inflation as well as rapid economic growth. In China, for example, wages rose by over 14% annually between 2000 and 2012. Assumptions about which parts of a company's expansion will be low cost might need to be revisited sooner than expected.

Labour laws

Labour laws can be one of the last things to change, even in a fast-modernising market. For example, more than 20 years after the collapse of the Soviet Union, labour regulations there are still not much changed from the Soviet era and heavily favour the employee. In India, labour laws have not been changed for 50 years; they make contract employees almost impossible to hire (so outsourced staff are deemed employees) and firing employees is extremely difficult. Many countries that perform well in other aspects for ease of doing business fall down on labour measures.

In Brazil, for example, companies often underestimate their labour obligations. When three businessmen bought a chain of pharmacies in Pernambuco in 1994, they were immediately taken to court by four former employees of the pharmacies who claimed they were owed R500,000 (then $570,000) for overtime and holidays. The new owners lacked the payroll records, and the labour court ruled against them – despite the fact that they had only just bought the business and the claimants had been in charge of payroll and work scheduling. It is essential when entering a market to get expert advice on labour regulations.

Employment protection regulations are especially important for companies undertaking an acquisition or a restructuring that might involve redundancies. And will it be possible to lay staff off in the event of a downturn? A lack of understanding might mean that the costs are much higher than expected.

Questions companies need to consider include the following:

- Statutory benefits. What benefits have to be paid beyond base salary? Mexico, for example, obliges companies to pay a Christmas bonus, plus a 10% share of profits.
- Employment standards. Are there any rules on who can be employed? In Turkey, the law mandates that companies must employ a certain number of disabled workers. As foreign companies often struggled to find people with the skills they needed, they would take on disabled people but not expect them to come into work.

- Working languages. Are there any restrictions on the languages that can be used to communicate with employees? Indonesia requires firms to conduct all formal communication with employees in Indonesian, and any employees who do not speak the language must be enrolled in classes.

- Visa rules. How accommodating are the regulations for transferring expats to the country? In Russia, working visas can take half a year to process – and it is far from certain that they will be renewed.

- Right to strike. Are workers allowed to join unions? And what rights are involved? In South Africa, for instance, these rights are wide-ranging, and in 2010 over 1m workers were on strike for several weeks over pay, with other unions holding sympathy stoppages.

- Redundancies. What is the process for handling redundancies, and how much compensation is likely to be due? In much of the former Soviet Union laying off workers is costly.

- Pay cuts. What leeway is there to reduce pay or other benefits in exchange for limiting redundancies? In Brazil, where labour laws are highly restrictive, there are tight controls on any reductions in salary.

- Injury compensation. What is your liability in the event of workplace injury or death? Chinese law requires companies to pay funeral subsidies of up to six months' wages, a monthly stipend of up to half the average wage and a one-off subsidy of up to 60 months' wages.

Workforce relations

Multinational companies may well be better employers than local companies, but it is important not to take it for granted that this will be understood. Employees in emerging markets may have little understanding of the conditions in multinational companies and can easily be taken in by scaremongering by local politicians or media. When Volkswagen, a German car company, was taking over Skoda in the former Czechoslovakia it initially found that although in most respects the deal was proceeding smoothly, it faced considerable opposition from unions – mainly on nationalist grounds. It turned this around by taking the trade union leaders to Germany to show them how the company operated: the training it gave, workplace conditions, and so on. The unions then switched to being firm supporters of the deal.

5 Infrastructure and property

IN THE DEVELOPED WORLD, good-quality infrastructure (including roads and rail) and public utilities (such as electricity, clean water, telephones and high-speed internet) are often taken for granted. In emerging markets, the situation can be very different. And don't be fooled by the state-of-the-art airports you may encounter on arrival in the capital – elsewhere, especially in rural areas, the infrastructure may well be patchy or falling apart. In China, India, Brazil, Mexico and South Africa, for example, the main cities and commercial centres may have world-class infrastructure, while towns and much of the countryside are underdeveloped. Costs, installation times and reliability of services can also vary widely – and be wildly inconsistent. A realistic assessment is crucial, because problems in these basic areas can bring a business to a standstill.

Transport services

Leading emerging markets are spending heavily on infrastructure, but they still have a lot of catching up to do. Many of them still cannot afford more than basic upgrades to roads, rail, power and telecommunications. And it is unwise to assume that infrastructure will always be maintained.

Poor infrastructure is often exacerbated by graft. In Cameroon, an *Economist* correspondent travelled with a beer truck on a 500km delivery run. It should have taken less than a day, but instead it took four days. It had to contend with 47 roadblocks (and many bribes), as well as flooded roads and a collapsed bridge. Only two-thirds of the load eventually reached the destination.

Where roads are good, congestion can be an even bigger problem than in the developed world. Car sales in big emerging markets are growing faster than the road network is expanding. In Istanbul the joke is that there are excellent flight connections – if you can get to the airport. One country manager there says she had come to accept that she would regularly miss flights because of traffic jams.

Distribution centres and warehouses are another big logistical challenge. An important question is how well they are adapted to local weather conditions. For example, in much of Asia Nestlé, a multinational food and beverage company, works with specialist distributors to make sure its chocolate does not melt before reaching the shops.

Ports are often among the first areas to be upgraded as a country opens up because they are essential for imports and exports. But inland the situation can be very different. Countries such as Egypt have developed-world-standard ports but lag far behind on road and rail infrastructure.

Nokia's experience at its manufacturing base near Chennai in India is illustrative. The factory has been a big success since it was set up in 2005, attracting many similar factories and suppliers to the area. The company has always had to make special arrangements to overcome infrastructure problems. It has its own generators in case of power cuts – its precision assembly process means that losing power even for a few seconds would result in the loss of hundreds of handsets. Nokia and other manufacturers in the area lay on bus services for workers because public transport is limited. But other problems are now arising as the local infrastructure becomes stretched. Increasing congestion on Chennai's roads is leading to delays and logistical problems. Airport infrastructure is not keeping up with rising demand. The local airport is small and outdated; it is being expanded, but proposals for a second airport with up to four runways are unlikely to be approved. Nokia's country manager says: "If government doesn't focus fast enough on infrastructure, it will definitely impact growth."

Do a thorough check-up

There is no substitute for visiting a country and seeing how easy it is to move around. There are also some other basic steps to help assess how hard it will be to move goods around:

- Look at ratings of transport infrastructure. The World Bank, for example, compiles a measure of logistics performance.
- Use toolkits. The World Bank also provides a trade and transport facilitation assessment toolkit.
- Dig a bit deeper into the data. The International Road Transport Union, for example, provides data on border-crossing times for trucks.
- Consult local specialists. Freight-forwarding firms, exporters, the port authorities and logistics providers are sources of useful information. Physical factors are one thing to check, but also ask about intangibles such as customs processes and likely delays.

Consider innovative solutions

Do not be discouraged by pot-holed roads, power blackouts or creaking communications. Businesses have found that they can still thrive through ingenuity, substitution and adaptation. Many multinational companies operate successfully in the face of some of the worst infrastructure in the world.

Selena Group, a manufacturer and distributor of construction chemicals, found that in Kazakhstan there was no trucking industry to speak of. It contacted bus companies that operated between the regional commercial centres, and they agreed to transport the company's goods. A senior manager at Selena says:

> The drivers were putting up a notice – no passengers. They were taking our goods, boxes of silicones, PEO forms, adhesives, and transporting the goods to the customers. It was a bit funny, I must admit, but it was an effective way of getting our goods to the customers.

Power supply

Rapid growth in demand for electricity, in combination with neglected networks and ageing power stations, is causing serious problems in many emerging markets. Urbanisation has a major impact on demand; Goldman Sachs has calculated that as the share of people living in cities rises by 1%, demand for electricity increases by 1.8%. Electricity capacity may need to increase by 140% in China and 80% in India over the next decade.

Countries are already struggling to keep up. In 2010, peak demand in India outstripped supply by almost 15%. Outside the cities, average availability of electricity is 12 hours a day, and even within cities supply is unreliable. In India, 600m Indians have no mains electricity at all while thousands of homes and businesses are forced to rely on their own power back-up system.

In assessing a company's energy needs, some basic steps are as follows:

- Review rankings of electricity and energy availability for the target market. The International Energy Agency, for example, provides data on electrification rates for both urban and rural areas.

- Assess the likely need for electricity over the short, medium and long term, based on growth expectations, and balance this against local supply.

- Consider whether energy use is centralised in a single site or more widespread. This can influence short-term strategies such as buying diesel generators.

Telecommunications and broadband

Emerging markets may be more sophisticated in their use of technology than expected. They often leapfrog old technologies. So countries where the fixed-line telecoms infrastructure is antiquated (or where it was never built at all) now have dense mobile networks. Countries that never had analogue television now have multi-channel digital satellite television. Some countries are largely bypassing the personal computer and moving straight to mobile devices.

However, although reasonable telecoms and broadband services are available in many emerging markets, penetration is much lower than in developed markets, in part because costs are often considerably higher. Usage patterns are also different. For mobile phones, for example, prepaid services are far more widely used than fixed contracts. And mobile phones are often shared – in rural Asia and Africa owners may even rent them out.

Successful senior managers of multinational companies in emerging markets must appreciate that, despite the relative poverty – or perhaps because of it – Asians, Africans and others are using technology in innovative ways to become more efficient consumers, or more profitable small businesses. Mobile communications and internet access (and often the two combined) have become the most significant delivery channels, more often than not of a single application: good old-fashioned cash. Mobile phone payments, through either transfers from relatives working overseas or point-to-point cashless transactions, have been a boon to consumers without bank accounts or regular access to a branch.

Countries such as Kenya or the Philippines (where mobile payment transactions topped $10 billion in 2012, roughly equal to 40% of the value of all consumer bank deposits in the country) have shown that emerging-market consumers can be better versed in advanced applications than their rich-world counterparts. Multinational business leaders who ignore fast-moving technology trends in poor countries, or assume technology levels must be below those of their home markets, do so to the detriment of their competitive position.

Land and real estate

Companies setting up in emerging markets may want to purchase land, especially if they are planning for the long term. But this can be a tricky area. For example, in India the government owns most of the land (which consequently is often underproductive and underutilised), so private land is in short supply and expensive. What is more, rules on the transfer or lease of land are outdated and unclear.

Land planning rules can cause big delays in proposed developments; and the rules vary considerably between markets.

Ernst & Young, a multinational professional services firm, has noted that in Russia it takes a year to get planning permission to build a factory – enough time to build and complete two factories in some other countries.

An acquisition or joint venture offers an immediate way of getting access to land or office space. But if a company needs to go it alone, leasing might make the most sense, at least initially. This is especially the case if the entry strategy is to put all the capital into gaining market share. And leasing is often quicker, giving an earlier start on building the business. Once there is a greater understanding of the market and the business proves successful, management can consider purchasing land or office space. When Siemens, a multinational engineering and electronics company, moved into India the process for obtaining land and setting up its factory was so complex that it decided to start out by renting an old shack while the process was completed – "that gave us a head-start of about two years", reckons one of its executives.

Of course, a company investing in building a factory will probably want to own the land. And the government might be willing to offer prime or discounted land to secure the investment. It is also worth checking what is happening with land prices. They are rising so rapidly in some of the main emerging markets, such as China, that latecomers are facing extremely high prices.

Kia Motors' investment in Slovakia in 2004 demonstrates how tricky the issue of land can be. The company had agreed a $1.3 billion investment in a giant new factory, and was ready to begin construction. This was the largest foreign investment in Slovakia for decades, and the government had fought hard to see off competition for the investment from neighbouring countries, especially Poland. It had promised to spend $730m on improving infrastructure around the site. But it did not own the site – ownership was divided among some 1,800 Slovaks, around half of whom refused to sell without being paid much more than was on offer. The dispute took a long time to resolve; so long that it almost derailed Kia's strategy.

Apart from the normal due diligence procedures for buying property, some other issues should be considered in an emerging market:

- Check if there are any claims on the land. In many emerging markets, there is a history of colonial and civil conflict leading to land appropriations. Are there any groups who claim the land you are buying as their own?

- Try to keep a low profile. As Kia found in Slovakia, if locals know the buyer is a large multinational, they might be inclined to demand a higher price.

- Have the authorities onside. Patience and persistence will be essential to negotiate the bureaucratic obstacles, but it may be possible to speed things up if government power is firmly on your side. The local, regional or national government will often make things happen, if they are convinced that the investment will benefit the country and the local community.

- Do not automatically go for an established hub. Setting up alongside other multinationals, or in an industry cluster, may well be beneficial. But it might be better to go elsewhere – the labour market may be less tight, operating costs might be lower, or land may be cheaper. And the government might offer more support if you are developing a new area.

6 Supply, distribution and marketing

Supply chains

In 1999, TCI, an Indian transport company, won a contract to supply Toyota's automobile factory in Bangalore. To comply with Toyota's "just-in-time" deliveries, TCI needed to make deliveries to the factory every two hours with over 99% reliability. That might be straightforward in Japan; but in India the poor state of the roads and congestion made it a daunting challenge. Furthermore, moving between India's 28 states and seven union territories can involve long border queues and bureaucratic obstacles. Drivers may be careless and unreliable, accidents are frequent, and the ageing lorries often break down. Rather than bring in a Japanese logistics company (as Japanese carmakers often like to do), Toyota trained TCI's drivers, for example to take care of their goods, drive sensibly and wear seatbelts. It monitored TCI, sometimes following its trucks, to make sure standards were being upheld. This allowed Toyota to stick to its just-in-time delivery model, reduced inventories and saved the company about $100m a year.

The main principle in supply chain management in emerging markets is that if what is needed does not exist, companies should be prepared to create it themselves. They must be innovative and adaptable. Many multinationals already have experience of integrating the world's leading emerging economies, such as China, into large and demanding supply chains.

Choosing suppliers

It often makes sense to source inputs locally; indeed, import tariffs or other regulations designed to encourage local sourcing may in effect give a company no choice. Some of the prices quoted might be surprisingly low. But price is not everything; reliability is also crucial. There is considerable reputational risk from product recalls, product safety and quality problems, so it is important to choose local suppliers carefully and work with them closely.

BASF supplies chemical products, many of which are highly combustible, and it knows it would be blamed if an accident happened involving its products. Joerg Wuttke, head of the company in China, comments on signing up a logistics partner:

> You really have to test the cars, test the trucks, see if the drivers have a valid driving licence, see how the tyres look, because if you just go by price you get an overworked, undereducated driver in a lousy truck and with bad wheels or tyres, and he has an accident, and then your name is in the media all over the place, you are in major trouble with the local government ... So you have to basically go the extra mile in order to make sure that your supply chain and logistics, in particular, are safeguarded. It costs more, but at the end it pays off because you have fewer accidents than your competitors.

Here are some questions to ask:

- Do we have the people and systems to manage an emerging-market supply chain effectively?
- Would we be better off integrating our new venture into our global supply network – if that is possible?
- How will we co-ordinate communication between our suppliers, partners and sub-suppliers?
- How can we be flexible, diversify risk and minimise the impact of supply disruptions?
- What are the social and environmental standards of our suppliers?
- What are their long-term record and corporate history?

Monitoring supply standards

After selecting a supplier, it is important to monitor them systematically to make sure they keep up the necessary standards. In 2010 Toyota sought to blame a series of accidents that led to the recall of millions of its vehicles on a supplier of accelerator-pedal assemblies. This did not work. Suppliers build parts to a car manufacturer's specifications, and it is the manufacturer's responsibility to ensure that standards are maintained. Toyota's reputation was badly damaged.

In emerging markets it is wise to go further than the standard supplier quality-assurance controls used in developed markets. This is not easy: setting standards is one thing, but ensuring compliance is another. Here are some things to do:

■ Undertake more frequent visits to the supplier's facilities.

■ Engage more with suppliers to strengthen their management techniques, working conditions and quality controls.

■ Create the expectation that the standards required in terms of speed, quantity or quality will be steadily raised.

■ Increase the level of testing, reporting and random sampling.

■ Make sure that the contract requires that you approve all subcontractors.

Integrating suppliers

If local suppliers create too many problems, there are some other strategies:

■ Set up a supplier business. For example, Starbucks concluded a deal in 2010 with the authorities in Yunnan province, China, to establish a local coffee-bean farm – its first ever.

■ Enter a joint venture with a local supplier. This will give you more control over the operation. For instance, Toyota has one with China's FAW Group to assemble the Prius.

■ Spread the risk. Apple and other high-tech firms use multiple suppliers in various emerging markets to ensure an uninterrupted supply of components and to undertake final assembly. This also reduces risks from political instability and natural disasters.

■ Invite a trusted supply partner from a different market to join you. Toyota has collaborated with a long-term partner, Mitsui, in its entry into a number of emerging markets, including China.

The manufacturing revolution

Perhaps the trend most commonly associated with globalisation has been the shift of manufacturing jobs from developed economies to lower-cost locations in Asia, and the emergence of China in particular as the new "workshop of the world". But as costs rise in emerging markets in line with growing prosperity, manufacturing is on the cusp of a new revolution, driven also by technological change, notably the emergence of 3D printing.

Automation versus low-cost labour

Wages in many emerging markets, especially in Asia, are rising rapidly. Those for Chinese manufacturing workers are going up by around 20% a year, faster than productivity is growing. The strengthening of the yuan has added to upward pressure on costs. India presents a similar picture. Growing labour unrest in China is also reducing the country's attractiveness as a base for manufacturing. One possible solution is to move to even lower-cost locations, and some production (for example, clothing and shoes) will shift to other low-wage countries in Asia, such as Bangladesh, Vietnam, Cambodia, Sri Lanka and Indonesia.

However, such moves are costly and time-consuming. With wages rising almost everywhere, companies are realising that this model has its limits, and they can no longer rely on the availability of large pools of cheap labour. Instead, many are prioritising improving labour productivity and are investing heavily in technology. Moving to greater automation means that there is less need to hire more workers, and that there is no need to regularly move manufacturing facilities. For example, Foxconn, a multinational electronic components manufacturer, announced in 2011 that it would place up to 1m robots in its Chinese factories by 2013 to undertake much of the work done until now by humans.

Reshoring, nearshoring, offshoring

While manufacturing wages in China and Asia have been rising rapidly, those in the US and Europe have been pretty much flat. The narrowing of the cost differential brings other factors back into play, such as skills, labour laws, infrastructure and the business environment. It also means that companies are more inclined to factor in the tangible and intangible costs of extended supply chains. These include the cost of shipping goods across the world, as well as the risk that natural disasters or political upheaval could cut off essential supplies. There are also benefits from proximity to end-markets for some kinds of production, as it allows quicker responsiveness and greater customisation. Companies have found that it is useful to be undertaking R&D in the same location as their manufacturing operations. This allows better cross-fertilisation of ideas, and production innovations often go hand-in-hand with breakthroughs in production techniques.

All in all, this means a trend towards reshoring. The US in particular stands to benefit from this trend because the cost of manufacturing there is falling. The production of shale gas has dramatically lowered the price of energy – a major consideration in manufacturing – and the dollar has weakened. The workforce is relatively flexible, and productivity continues to improve. As a result, in a survey of large US manufacturers by Boston Consulting Group in spring 2012, nearly two-fifths said they were either planning to move or thinking about moving production facilities from China back to the US. The situation for Continental European firms is a little different because there was less offshoring in the first place; it was more difficult and expensive than in the US to shut down production at home because of labour laws and political pressure.

Alongside reshoring there will also be a rise in nearshoring, which will especially benefit central and eastern Europe (CEE) and Mexico as locations for supplying west European and North American markets respectively. Manufacturing investment in these countries over the past decade was curtailed by rising costs compared with Asia, but this is now changing. Average wages for Mexican workers, for example, are only slightly higher than for Chinese ones, and goods from Mexico can be trucked to North America in days, rather than spending months being shipped. At the same time, Mexico and CEE are still cheaper for manufacturing than the US and western Europe. Companies are also rethinking where to manufacture to serve important growth markets outside Asia, such as Russia and the Middle East and North Africa.

One CEE regional manager at an electronics multinational illustrated the trend:

We're shifting business back from China because of cost developments there. Particularly in the B2B segment we're moving production back to Poland. This allows us to have a short lead time for orders and customise more. It also reduces our exposure to delays. You don't have to wait 8–10 weeks while your inventories are at sea, with no way to intervene or adapt them.

Advanced manufacturing techniques

The trends towards greater automation and reshoring/nearshoring will also be boosted by advanced manufacturing techniques that will allow firms to make production even less labour-intensive. The most important of these is additive manufacturing, popularly known as 3D printing, which uses a digital description of an object to build it in physical form, layer by layer. 3D printing is already being used in R&D to make prototypes, and is now ready to be applied to production as well – making aircraft and car parts, and household electronics, for example. It renders traditional economies of scale redundant, as each item can be changed at little or no extra cost. This will make it more economical, and also more important, for firms to produce in proximity to final markets.

Global manufacturing

All this does not imply a mass switch of manufacturing away from Asia. For one thing, China benefits from an excellent supply of components and good infrastructure. More importantly, though, it is now a major market in its own right. What the changes in manufacturing really mean is that firms will move away from a model of manufacturing everything in one low-cost place to supply the rest of the world. Rather than offshoring, companies will design their manufacturing footprint to balance cost efficiency with the need to be as close as possible to key markets globally – to be onshore in as many places as possible. The manufacturing revolution will allow firms to produce close to developed-world markets again, but they will also want to manufacture in proximity to increasingly important final markets in the emerging world.

Distribution

A 2012 survey by Global Intelligence Alliance of 39 global consumer and retail companies cited distribution and access to customers as the number one factor for the success of their emerging-market ventures, way ahead of a country's economic and demographic profile.

The headache of getting goods to customers begins, of course, with getting shipments across borders. In OECD high-income countries it takes just ten days to import or export and costs around $1,000 per container. In eastern Europe and Central Asia it costs more than double and takes nearly three times as long. In South Asia and in sub-Saharan Africa it is even worse (see Table 1.1).

TABLE 1.1 **Trading across borders**

	Documents to export (no.)	Time to export (days)	Cost to export ($ per container)	Documents to import (no.)	Time to import (days)	Cost to import ($ per container)
OECD high-income	4	10	1,028	5	10	1,080
East Asia & Pacific	6	21	923	7	22	958
Eastern Europe & Central Asia	7	26	2,134	8	29	2,349
Latin America & Caribbean	6	17	1,268	7	19	1,612
Middle East & North Africa	6	19	1,083	8	22	1,275
South Asia	8	32	1,603	9	33	1,736
Sub-Saharan Africa	8	31	1,990	9	37	2,567

Source: World Bank, Doing Business 2013

Compounding the problem, transit times are unpredictable,

making it difficult to smooth downstream supply chains and challenging to manage exchange-rate risk – the volatility of emerging-market currencies makes hedging expensive and in many cases exchange-based solutions for currency hedging might not exist at all. Some firms are able to mitigate some of these risks by producing locally, but for many multinationals scale rules out this option.

Once goods have cleared customs, other problems emerge, beginning with the transport network. In most of Africa, for example, the road network is woefully inadequate and typically in poor repair; the rail network is generally not a serious option at all. This is changing, and progress, though slow, is inexorable.

Another challenge is that, in the developing world, less than half of the population lives in urban areas. Private companies and NGOs alike have come up with innovative solutions for going the very last mile to reach rural consumers, but even reaching urban consumers is daunting. Fortunately, in the long term, the rapid pace of urbanisation in emerging markets will tip the balance: by 2020, more than half of the developing-world population will be living in towns and cities.

Meanwhile, businesses face another type of challenge when it comes to reaching their customers in emerging markets, where traditional retail is still dominant; even in Brazil and China, such retail still has a market share of 60%. And within traditional retail, it is "nano-stores" – a term coined by Edgar Blanco and Jan Fransoo of Eindhoven University of Technology* – that set the tone. A nano-store is smaller than a convenience store, or mini-store, which has between 15 and 40 square metres of shopping surface. Nano-stores are tiny: smaller than a small room, and often just run from a street cart. But there are an estimated 50m of these entities serving 5 billion customers in emerging markets, so global companies would do well to think about how to ensure their products are on offer.

Some companies are already there. Blanco and Fransoo report that in Mexico, Coca-Cola supplies 1.2m points of sale, while in Mexico City alone Unilever delivers ice cream to more than 10,000 freezer units. Distributing in this way requires models that are essentially different from those used in modern retail environments.

---

* http://cms.ieis.tue.nl/Beta/Files/WorkingPapers/wp_404.pdf

Choosing and managing distributors

Most global companies respond to the challenge by outsourcing distribution and the associated headaches, as do regional and local manufacturers which may lack the capital or scale to do things more directly. In most emerging markets companies will be lining up to become distributors. Here are some considerations to help choose between them:

- Visit their facilities; inspect their vehicles and systems.
- Interview the managers and assess their technical expertise.
- Check their financial record.
- Talk to their current and past customers.
- Talk to the retailers they supply.
- Make sure they have sufficient geographic reach.
- Check whether their performance indicators are realistic.

A company needs to communicate its long-term goals to its distributors and encourage them to become long-term partners. If they see a promising future distributing the company's goods, they are more likely to adapt to its needs and work to meet its targets.

Ideally, a company needs to have its own people on the ground to work closely with the distributors and monitor their performance. Yum! Restaurants in India, for example, makes regular quality audits of all its distributors. A large part of its distribution is temperature-controlled, so temperature data loggers are installed in all cold vehicles as well as cold warehouses. And products are checked at the unloading point in warehouses and at store.

Creating a distribution network

However, going through an intermediary can limit the relationship building needed to develop a company's brand and deepen its understanding of customers. That in itself places a serious limit on the effectiveness of marketing. Moreover, it may not be able to find a full-service national distribution company – there are none in India, for example – which means that outsourcing distribution can consume a lot of resources. Harit Nagpal, CEO of Tata Sky, says:

[In India] you need to deal with thousands of such distributors across the country, each one being an independent entity. You need to go and appoint each one of these separately, set terms with each one of them and then have your own people supervise their activity.

An alternative is for companies to create their own distribution network. Caterpillar, for example, usually relies heavily on its network of dealers, but in Russia it could not find a suitable partner and so decided to handle it itself. There are a few possible approaches:

- buy a fleet of trucks and vans and create your own distribution network;
- ask a distributor used in your home country to expand into the new market alongside you;
- buy a distributor and tailor it to your needs.

It is also worth looking at what works in other emerging markets. Different approaches include creating distribution alliances with other companies and sharing warehouse space. The most important thing is to be flexible and adapt to local conditions.

Marketing

It is important to localise the company's branding. Products and services are increasingly likely to be adapted to local conditions too (see innovation and R&D below). Even brands with high global recognition are localised to some extent, because they have to translate their names, slogans and other marketing into different languages. This is not always straightforward. When Coca-Cola entered China, its name had no literal translation, so the company had to find a set of Mandarin characters that were phonetically similar.

There are many possible pitfalls that can be avoided only through local fluency and awareness. Nike's "flaming air" logo on its Nike Air trainers, for example, was replaced in Arabic markets because it looked similar to the Arabic term for Allah.

Sometimes, however, a company's brand will be desired precisely because it is foreign, and it is important to know the limits to a localisation approach. A Coca-Cola advert in Russia that incorporated

Coke into a Russian fairy tale irritated many viewers, who felt that the US product had no place in a quintessentially Russian story.

Flexibility will therefore be needed. Companies often tackle this by establishing brand principles that must be maintained, while giving local offices some leeway to shape an offering or message that is relevant to their market.

Getting Oreo right

Sanjay Khosla is president of developing markets at Mondelēz International, a multinational confectionery, food and beverage conglomerate, formerly Kraft Foods. One crucial question he asks of the company's brands is: "How do you get the balance right between mindlessly global and hopelessly local?" The company's experience with Oreo provides a good example. It is the largest biscuit brand in the world, and had its 100th birthday in 2012. For 95 years, Oreo's success was mainly in the US, and attempts to make it work elsewhere failed spectacularly. Khosla says:

> Five years back when I went to China, it was clear that our approach was not working. In fact, Oreo was close to being delisted. For the Chinese consumer we learned that Oreo was too sweet, too big and the price points were too high. Why? Simply because very often, what is good for the US may not be good for China and what's good for China may not be good for Brazil. We gave the team a blank cheque … an unlimited resource to do something with Oreo.

The China team made Oreos less sweet and introduced new forms like wafers, at lower price points. They used local marketing, within the global Oreo positioning. And they acted as entrepreneurs – although with the advantages of a multinational's scale and expertise. As a result, Mondelēz introduced locally relevant flavours like green tea and strawberry. Once nearly delisted, Oreo is now the number one biscuit in China.

This approach was followed across other markets, innovating for local tastes, and using global technology and procurement without changing the global brand positioning. Mondelēz now has blueberry ice cream Oreos in the Philippines, orange ice cream Oreos in Indonesia and *dulce de leche* Oreos in

Argentina. As a result, Oreo has surged from being a roughly $200m brand in emerging markets in 2006 to a $1 billion brand in 2012. Khosla says:

Lessons learned: focus and put extraordinary resource and talent behind where you want to win. Give teams blank cheques to unleash the potential of their people. We have found that when you get talent to act as owners, they become even more commercially accountable. Blank cheques don't always work; the important thing is to do and learn. And if you have more successes than failures, you are OK.

Khosla suggests that many companies are seduced by the 1 billion or so people in China and India and get into trouble because they don't have a sustainable business model:

Five years back our business in China was in a classic vicious cycle: small, unprofitable and with low gross margins. And there was no point in scaling up something that was not working. We changed our approach and focused the business on a few things where we could win. We fixed the business model with a cost structure where we could compete locally. And we doubled our innovation rate. We invested in building depth of local talent. Recruiting ahead of need. This is a critical part of the equation as everyone is now investing in high-growth markets. And we gave the China team a blank cheque to dream big, act as entrepreneurs and owners. Our China business is now profitable. In fact, we are now one of the fastest growing CPG [consumer packaged goods] companies in China today.

7 Innovation and R&D

EMERGING MARKETS will be the main source of growth for multinationals over the coming years. So it makes sense for them to focus innovation efforts on these markets, rather than adapting products that have been developed for rich-world customers. They will often be competing with highly innovative and well-resourced local competitors who are well-attuned to the needs of their domestic customers. If Western multinationals do not come up with innovations in emerging markets (and then take them global), their emerging-market competitors will. There are two main trends: reverse innovation and frugal innovation.

Frugal innovation

Frugal innovation involves the adoption of low-cost, efficient processes and technologies to create products and services that are affordable for emerging-market customers. This does not mean just stripping products down to basic, no-frills versions; companies must design products from scratch, then redesign their R&D, manufacturing and distribution processes to fit their new customers' needs.

Emerging-market companies are leading the way. Companies such as Tata Group, Infosys and Wipro, all Indian multinationals, are used to operating in an environment of constrained capital, technology and resources. This forces them to think carefully about the innovation process and find ingenious ways to cut costs and overcome hurdles. For example, BYD, a Chinese electronics firm, succeeded in reducing costs of lithium-ion batteries from $40 to under $12. Godrey & Boyce Manufacturing, an Indian group, developed a $70 refrigerator, the Chotukool, which runs on batteries.

Anil Gupta has noted three principal steps in frugal innovation:

- Design from scratch. A study by the Rand Corporation found that in the West some 70–75% of the cost is locked in by the design. Innovation is then just around the margins. But by starting from scratch the 70–75% becomes a variable again.
- Leverage the local conditions. This means minimising the add-on costs of selling the product.
- Localise the cost structure. In emerging economies the local cost structure is generally low, and so logistics costs are lower.

Reverse innovation

Reverse innovation involves innovations developed primarily for emerging markets but then exported to developed markets. GE, a multinational conglomerate, for example, has for a long time produced high-tech medical devices for hospitals in developed markets, but these are generally not affordable in poor emerging markets. Also, most of the population in countries such as India and Bangladesh live in rural areas, where there are few hospitals. The device has to come to the patient, rather than vice versa.

So GE invented a low-cost, portable electrocardiogram (ECG) machine, the Mac 400, which can run on batteries (important in areas without reliable electricity). It sells for around $500, a fraction of the cost of a traditional ECG machine. GE has found that the device can also be sold in developed markets when more bulky devices are unsuitable. For example, ambulance services in the US use a slightly modified version of the Mac 400 at accident sites or to assess patients en route to hospital.

Reverse innovation is a growing trend. It usually costs much less to research and launch a product in an emerging market than in a developed one. Thus companies are likely to prefer to experiment in emerging markets before deciding whether to roll out a product elsewhere in the world.

Adapting products for local conditions

Innovation for emerging markets does not necessarily have to be radical to succeed, however. Sometimes, adapting an existing product to suit local tastes in emerging markets is all that is needed. Unilever, for example, sells more than 100 variants of its Lux soap brand around the world. Coca-Cola adjusts the taste and sweetness of its flagship Coke product depending on the preferences of the local market, switching between cane sugar and corn syrup, for instance. The key is to recognise when adaptation will not work and innovation is required instead. Larger companies often use a combination of the two approaches.

Relocating R&D

Innovating for emerging markets also requires companies to think about where to conduct research and development (R&D). Multinationals increasingly recognise that they must locate more of their R&D facilities in emerging markets, both to get closer to their customers and to take advantage of the skills available. In practice, this means rethinking their entire approach to R&D. Rather than being concentrated in a single market, the process is becoming diffuse.

R&D investment in emerging markets has already increased considerably. GE, for example, spent over $50m on a huge R&D centre in Bangalore for its health-care division, and announced in 2010 that it would build an R&D centre in Brazil to serve Latin America. The 2010 Global Innovation 1000 report by Booz & Company, a consultancy, found that R&D spending in India and China increased by 42% in 2009, while spending in North America, Japan and Europe fell. More than 1,200 multinational companies now operate R&D facilities in China, according to the Chinese Ministry of Commerce.

But even while seeking to expand their share of sales in emerging markets, many multinationals have been slow to adapt their innovation processes to this new reality. This is often because of concerns about giving up control. R&D is an expensive, uncertain process that is crucial for a company's future. Management may struggle with the idea of handing it over to engineers in emerging markets, or decentralising it in multiple centres.

The process can be divided into four stages:

- Western and centralised. Traditionally, a company centralises its R&D at corporate headquarters. It may have more than one centre, but these will invariably be in developed markets.

- A toe in the water. The company hands over some aspects of the process to engineers in emerging markets, but often only basic ones, and with the aim of reducing costs rather than developing products for local consumption.

- Responding to market needs. With the realisation that emerging markets are important sources of growth that need dedicated products and services, the company hands over increasingly high-value R&D work to local engineers. But although they receive more autonomy, overall responsibility for innovation still rests with corporate headquarters.

- The polycentric approach. Breaking with the traditional centralised model, corporate headquarters no longer has complete control over R&D. Instead, there are multiple innovation hubs in strategic markets, in both developed and emerging economies. Each hub's main responsibility is to create innovations for the market it is in; these may then be taken up by other markets globally. Duplication of effort can be avoided by having the hubs connected in a loose network.

At present, only a handful of companies fully embrace polycentric innovation. The term was coined by Navi Radjou, executive director of the Centre for India and Global Business at Judge Business School at the University of Cambridge. He highlights John Deere, a tractor manufacturer, Cisco, a technology company, and Obopay, a mobile technology company, as leading proponents.

Creating a global R&D function

Although many companies have accepted that they must invest more in R&D in emerging markets, they often still find integrating a global innovation programme difficult. One challenge is how far to delegate decision-making. Excessive centralisation may restrict creativity, but too much decentralisation could duplicate effort. Collaboration across the company needs to be systematically encouraged to make sure that ideas are shared.

In 2008 Unilever reorganised its global R&D operation. Previously it had an unwieldy structure of separate innovation groups for food, home and personal care, and corporate research, based at various R&D centres around the world. The new structure was designed to create simplicity and efficiency. There is now just one Unilever R&D organisation with six "strategic sites", intended to provide "a global expertise base from which it will deliver an integrated research programme". This structure reports to one new position: chief R&D officer.

Unilever tilts towards co-ordination. Others may put more emphasis on autonomy, and making the most of a local R&D lab's understanding of its market. Google, for example, gives its R&D offices globally a high degree of autonomy, while encouraging close collaboration with other locations by placing individual projects in these local offices within bigger global research initiatives.

Another solution is to think of R&D centres as innovation hubs. Placing these centres in priority emerging markets, and then seeking commonalities across other markets, allows companies to ensure economies of scale.

Intellectual property protection

Another reason some companies are reluctant to undertake R&D in emerging markets is the risk of intellectual property theft. Motorola invested heavily in R&D in China, but found that its corporate secrets were leaking away. Workers would join the company, learn the technology, and then take their knowledge to a local Chinese firm. As Motorola's former chief technology officer, Dennis Roberson, told the *Pittsburgh Tribune-Review*:

> Motorola was used as a training ground for all the competitors in China. A person might work for you for six months or a year, and then go over to a Chinese competitor ... Things like a two-year non-compete clause don't work well in China.

In 2010 Motorola filed a civil lawsuit against 14 people and two companies for conspiracy and misappropriation of business secrets. Companies need to have a strategy that manages this risk. Some put considerable effort into screening employees to identify potential risks of theft.

8   Ethics and competition

Bribery and corruption

Corruption and how to tackle it have always been significant concerns for businesses in emerging markets. But as firms deepen their roots outside their home markets and empower local operations or subsidiaries, they are more exposed to corruption than ever before – and the stakes are inherently higher. What constitutes corruption? And what are some best practices for dealing with it?

The US Foreign Corrupt Practices Act (FCPA) came into effect in 1977 to crack down on companies that bribed foreign officials. The landmark legislation was the first of its kind in the world. Previously, bribes and corruption were treated as legitimate costs of doing business outside US borders.

In December 1997, 35 countries signed the OECD's Anti-Bribery Convention, committing them to passing legislation that criminalises bribery of foreign public officials. By 2013, 40 countries had signed up – the latest being Colombia in December 2012 – and all have passed laws making such bribery a crime.

Indeed, over the past few decades the legislative framework governing corruption has been strengthened. The FCPA and the UK's Anti-Bribery Act both now include not just the direct bribery of foreign public officials but also indirect bribery, through partners or intermediaries. This means that a company is responsible not only for its own actions, but also for those of even loosely affiliated partners.

Although national policies on corruption and bribery are more stringent than in the past, enforcement remains mixed. This is partly because of the difficulty of proving bribery when sophisticated money-laundering techniques are used. According to the OECD, as of December 2011, only 300 companies or individuals had faced criminal proceedings for foreign bribery in the states that had signed the Anti-Bribery Convention.

Corruption remains rampant

Meanwhile, corruption remains rampant throughout the world – in emerging and mature markets alike. Not one of the 176 countries included in Transparency International's 2012 Corruption Perceptions Index earns a perfect (completely corruption-free) score of 100. While many western European – particularly Nordic – countries are listed at the less-corrupt top of the index, the big emerging markets have significant room for improvement: Brazil ranks 69th, China 80th, India 94th and Russia 133rd.

Although Western companies are under more scrutiny than ever before, they report that bribery is endemic in many high-growth markets around the world. For example, local officials expect payment for licences in Russia; drug approvals come at a cost in China; and it is widely known that imports into Nigerian ports can languish if customs officials' pockets are not lined. And while most companies tout their zero-tolerance policies, a handful of high-profile cases against some of the world's largest multinationals over the past few years reveal that many have significant room for improving compliance.

In 2006 German regulators announced that the country's industrial giant Siemens was under investigation for paying bribes to public officials around the world. The ensuing case brought a corporate culture that condoned corruption into the limelight. Siemens eventually paid around $2 billion in fines to both the German and US governments – making this the most expensive corruption scandal to date. (In the meantime, the firm has become a model for cleaning up its operations.)

A year after Siemens settled its case, two US companies, KBR (engineering, construction and private military contracting) and Halliburton (oilfield services and construction), were jointly fined $579m for bribing Nigerian officials to win construction contracts. In 2012 the US Securities and Exchange Commission (SEC) charged

Pfizer, a pharmaceuticals company, with making payments in exchange for regularity approval in countries from China to Russia and Italy. Walmart, one of the world's largest retailers, is in the throes of a scandal involving payment to officials in Mexico in exchange for altered zoning maps. According to the *New York Times*, Walmart's own internal investigations into FCPA violations now extend beyond Mexico to China, India and Brazil.

Tackling the problem

These cases demonstrate how costly unethical business practices can be: both to a company's balance sheet and, more importantly, to its long-term reputation. Here are some best practices for dealing with corruption and ensuring staff in global subsidiaries and partners understand that compliance is paramount:

- Training: communicate compliance policies. All employees throughout the world should be trained on compliance policies. They need to understand exactly what constitutes corruption – the difference between a bribe and a gift, for example – and that bribes are not always as straightforward as they might think. Does a payment for an expedited licence violate compliance policies? Perhaps. Companies must also make it clear that no business is better than unethical business. While all units around the world are undoubtedly under pressure to hit their targets, companies need to infuse into the corporate culture the idea that it is better to miss a target because of lost business through refusing to pay a bribe than to break compliance rules.

- Take internal controls seriously. Internal policing is the best way to guarantee ethical business. When corruption is suspected, companies should conduct thorough investigations and report any wrongdoings to the authorities. Many companies have got into trouble over the past few years by trying to conceal cases of bribery or corruption. This sends the wrong message to the entire company, and makes leadership seem complicit. External auditors can provide objective perspectives and help eliminate any temptation to conceal possible violations of the FCPA, the Anti-Bribery Act, or any other national laws.

■ Zero tolerance means more than zero. While corruption has long been blamed on greedy public officials throughout emerging markets, ultimately bribery is a two-way transaction. Zero tolerance needs to be a constant message from a firm's senior management all the way down the corporate ladder. Encourage whistle-blowing and set examples.

Corporate responsibility

It is getting harder to operate successfully in emerging markets without putting sustainability and responsibility at the core of a company's operations. Despite this, there are still regional chief executives who believe (privately, of course) that far too much time and money are spent on corporate sustainability and responsibility (CSR) programmes, indicating a serious dislocation between enlightened head offices and regional hubs. In other cases, it is the global head office that fails to grasp the need for interventions and practices that would be irrelevant or superfluous in developed markets where the adequacy of physical and social infrastructure is taken for granted.

Failure of traditional CSR

CSR is still widely taken to refer to corporate social responsibility, but this concept has come under increasing attack in the past decade. A leading thinker on the subject, Wayne Visser, argues that CSR as most of us know it has failed:[*]

> Most sustainability and corporate responsibility programs are about being less bad rather than good. They are about selective and compartmentalised "programs" rather than holistic and systemic change.

Thus CSR may take the form of ad-hoc interventions that are defensive and typically are implemented to satisfy the most basic regulatory requirements or avoid penalties, such as employee volunteer programmes or targeted spending.

Philanthropy and charitable programmes are one step further up the value chain towards a systemic approach, and are probably the most widespread form of implementation, leaking into promotional programmes that seek to

---

*Wayne Visser, "The Ages and Stages of CSR – Towards the future with CSR 2.0", CSR International Paper Series, No. 3, 2011.

use corporate philanthropy to enhance the brand. Some companies take a far more integrated approach, often referred to as "corporate social investment" or "creating shared value", which is close to the most mature stage, where a company incorporates sustainability and responsibility into the heart of its business models and products.

Visser's view is that traditional CSR has failed because it was incremental in nature and simply not of a scale to make any real difference to the problems being targeted. Lack of commitment from senior management – because CSR is perceived as peripheral to the "real" business – is another cause of failure, probably because responsible behaviour brings few short-term rewards of a type that would excite financial markets. Lastly, it is hard to make a compelling general business case for CSR: there are exceptions to the rule – which prove it – but the reality is that short-term efficiency gains are likely to be marginal. CSR is a long-term game. For it to be effective, our thinking needs an overhaul, and practice needs to shift, at both macro and micro levels.

Making CSR work

Because of this, best practice is to define CSR strategy at global company level, but with considerable autonomy in local implementation – guided by both global principles and local needs and realities.

Dow's Southern Africa programme

One example of this is the approach of Dow, a multinational chemical company, to sustainability and its manifestation in southern Africa, where skills development forms a core part of the strategy. Thus the company – which has a number of manufacturing operations in the region – has upgraded the skills of all employees, ensuring that every member of staff is functionally literate. All staff have access to the internet and also receive support for further education. As an aside, ensuring that employees' children receive a decent education is often cited as an excellent way not just to improve the talent pool in the longer term, but also to decrease staff turnover.

By providing a mobile science laboratory and trained tutors at a local science centre, Dow Southern Africa also supports the delivery of science education to high-school students at underserved schools in a community near one of its plants. These are just a couple of aspects of a skills development programme that also includes providing university scholarships for science students.

The strategy is driven by far more than the simple desire to be a good corporate citizen; investing in this way also helps to create a talent pool in the not-too-distant future, from which candidates for global, as well as local, positions can be drawn.

Nestlé's CSV approach

Nestlé adopted the approach of creating shared value (CSV) in 2006. Investments focus on three areas that are core to the company's business activities and underpin its value chain: nutrition, water and rural development. It has been able to do this by building on a strong base of compliance and environmental sustainability, extending the approach from how it does business internally to how it interacts with the communities it works in and engages in social and economic development.

One example of this is helping smallholder dairy farmers in southern Africa to scale up to commercial production levels by assisting them with advice, equipment and purchase agreements. Another is the Nestlé R&D centre in Abidjan, Côte d'Ivoire, which is developing high-quality seedlings to improve the quality and quantity of cocoa produced by smallholder farmers, thereby improving their livelihoods as well as ensuring a healthy supply chain. Another feature of the strategy is to encourage the development of innovative social enterprises through an annual CSV prize, which endows the winner with Sfr500,000 ($546,000) to scale up their business.

An important aspect of the Nestlé approach is the alignment with national development frameworks and, more generally, with the UN's Millennium Development Goals. Other companies share this aim, but in some cases, it is at odds with how other parts of the business might operate. For example, a large African gold-mining company aims to align its African CSR programme north of South Africa with the Millennium Development Goals but recently admitted failing to communicate with workers in South Africa, having abdicated this responsibility to the trade unions. Less than a week after the admission was made public it announced the decision to dispose of assets where industrial unrest had occurred.

Longer-term imperatives

Businesses operating in emerging markets are usually hampered by higher operating risks and challenges that are alien to developed countries. Aligning CSR in a thoughtful way is unlikely to help improve any bottom lines in the short term, but building a business in new markets is not a short-term game. The value that a creative and well-implemented strategy can create for all stakeholders certainly requires long-term, consistent commitment.

Competition

Increased global interest in emerging markets naturally turns up the competitive heat from two different sources, each of which creates a particular threat for global firms. The first is from other multinationals, all equally hungry for yield from higher-growth markets in Asia, Latin America and Africa. For example, many foreign retailers in the China market – such as Zara, a Spanish clothing retailer, and Lawson, a Japanese convenience store chain – expect 20–25% of their global revenues to come from there within the next ten years. Zara aims to open some 200 stores annually in China over the next three years and Lawson some 10,000 stores during this decade, roughly as many as it has in Japan.

The second source is business from emerging markets. Disregarding the potential for unfair business practices or protectionist policies from governments favouring "local champions", the real competitive threat comes from domestic businesses, great and small, which understand customers, distribution networks and marketing strategies, often (if not usually) better than foreign entrants. For example, Hangzhou Wahaha, a Chinese beverage-maker, has built a $5.2 billion business against competition from the likes of Coca-Cola and PepsiCo by targeting rural areas, filling local product gaps, keeping costs low and emphasising its Chinese origins.

In many respects, local companies are difficult to compete with. For example, a senior executive at an electronics multinational in Poland says:

SMEs are now key competitors in the local market. We have backward engineered their products – everything's the same as ours except the cost price. They're operating with low or no margin!

Multinational companies may face some other challenges from local companies:

- They may have cheaper production costs. They will invariably pay less for inputs, their quality, hygiene and safety standards will probably be lower, and they may treat their staff poorly. Whatever the reason, multinationals will find it hard or impossible to match their prices.
- They can often adapt much more quickly, particularly if multinationals have to run everything through head office. They have a deep understanding of the market, whereas multinationals may still be struggling to work out what it really wants.
- They often excel at cheap but effective marketing, perhaps accessing poor or rural customers who are beyond multinationals' reach. And they may take advantage of multinationals' efforts to create awareness of new product categories.
- They are not impeded by the need for compliance with Western anti-corruption legislation.
- Patriotism sells, and they will constantly play this card.
- Many emerging-market companies are sophisticated and well run. They copy foreign best practice whenever relevant. One company in Bulgaria had an arrangement with a retired US manager, who visited every few months to advise on how to improve its management practices.

Global competitors

Competition from emerging-market companies is not just local: many are now preparing to go global. Shane Tedjarati, president of global high-growth regions at Honeywell, says:

It's the desire of every Chinese company. As soon as they get to a few million dollars, you walk in their corridors and you see a map of the world with plans for how they are going to conquer it continent by continent.

So another important reason why multinational companies cannot ignore emerging markets is that they will increasingly bring new competition to home markets of Western multinationals, especially through new products and ways of doing business.

Rapid growth in domestic markets means that emerging-world companies can develop quickly to a stage where they can contemplate international expansion. Some 20% of the *Fortune* Global 500 are already emerging-market companies – Chinese, Indian, Brazilian, Russian, South Korean and Turkish firms all feature. Global telecom giants Huawei and ZTE from China, and the expansive conglomerate Tata from India, are examples of emerging-market firms that have expanded rapidly abroad (the two Chinese companies each operate in over 150 countries). The EIU expects foreign direct investment outflows from China alone to surge from $17 billion in 2007 to $170 billion in 2017.

Big Cola, a Peruvian-made soft drink, already a fixture among consumers across South America, is now one of the fastest growing cola brands in India, Vietnam and Indonesia. Price points and packaging formats are crucial to its increasing Asian success; in Big Cola's case (and as the company's brand implies) this means the opposite of the common strategy of creating smaller versions of existing products that are sold to value-conscious families.

Emerging-market firms are often well-capitalised, fast moving and keen to increase their global market share, using their understanding of emerging-market needs. They are exploiting their experience of low-cost production to compete strongly with their developed-world counterparts in low-cost segments and moving upwards as quality improves. Companies from the emerging world will one day actively shape Western consumer habits, as did East Asian companies such as Samsung, Sony and Nintendo a generation before. Perhaps a sign that emerging markets have really arrived will be when one of them makes a hit product that everyone wants, as Japan did in the 1980s with the Sony Walkman.

Emerging-market multinationals will also pursue expansion through acquisition – not just to gain growth in other markets, but also technology, know-how and established Western brands. This trend has already been seen in emerging-market sovereign-wealth funds, and companies from these countries are now likely to follow. The purchase of IBM's computer-manufacturing business for $1.75 billion by Lenovo, a Chinese computer-maker, in 2004 is an early example. Now China's Geely owns Volvo and India's Tata owns Jaguar and Land Rover.

Tackling the competition

The first step a company should take is to learn everything it can about the competition, with the aim of finding out how it can do something different, better, or more cheaply. This means working like a detective, doing as much quality research as possible. Speaking to former employees and customers of local competitors, and testing competing products and services, will also provide valuable insights.

Honeywell has a strategy of "becoming the Chinese competitor". As Tedjarati says:

> In every respect from R&D, marketing, people, channel – becoming the absolute local competitor means that we can beat the actual local competitors, especially the Chinese competitors, at their game ... And the better, the savvier China operators we become, the better we are with dealing with them in other turfs.

This means fundamentally changing the way the company operates and its mindset. Then the business needs to be adapted and strategies deployed that allow for quick defence and sustained offence on an increasingly crowded playing field. This will be discussed in more detail in Chapter 10.

9　Entering the market

ONCE A COMPANY HAS DECIDED it wants to be in a country, there are tactical questions to face. Is it better to proceed cautiously and build up gradually, or make a big push straight away, with higher risk but potentially higher reward? Should the company make an acquisition or go it alone? Commitment from the top is crucial, and it helps to have realistic budgets and expectations – succeeding in an emerging market is often more challenging than managers think it will be. Some sort of local presence is also essential.

Modes of entry

The best way to enter a market depends on a company's business, the nature of the market and the timing. But at the very least the company will, ideally, establish a one-person office to provide sales and marketing support, and to represent it locally. Distributors and agents can help considerably, but relying on them carries brand and reputational risks. If there is no physical presence, then sooner or later either the business will fail, or it will develop in ways that do not fit the company's goals.

A decision needs to be made on which operational model will work best: for example, joint venture, acquisition, brownfield, greenfield, appointed distributor or agency, franchise. The key is to be flexible and adaptable – the same approach will not work everywhere. And the operating model for a country will probably need to evolve. What is needed to enter the market is not always what is needed to prosper in the longer term. For example, a joint venture might be the best option initially, but later it may make more sense to switch to a fully owned subsidiary.

Joint ventures

A survey by Deloitte, a professional services firm, found that joint ventures with local companies are the most popular model for emerging-market entry, chosen in nearly 40% of cases. One reason for their popularity is that a joint venture can help a company quickly gain local expertise. They can also provide contacts, which are crucial in emerging markets. As well as influence with politicians and regulators, the local partner may be able to offer established supplier relationships, a distribution network, a product portfolio and a loyal network of customers – which could take years to create for an entrant going it alone.

There may be no alternative in any case. Many emerging markets have foreign-investment rules that require joint ventures. In India, for instance, regulations in the retail sector in effect forced Tesco, a multinational retailer, to enter into a joint venture in order to get into the market. Or well-established local brands or a complex market might make it impossible to succeed by starting at the bottom alone.

But joint ventures are never easy and can create major headaches. For example:

- The local partner probably will not be able to match the company's financial heft. That could hinder expansion.

- Objectives will often differ. The company might have a gradual, long-term growth strategy in which it would eventually buy out the local partner, while the local partner is after quick profits. Or their real aim might be to get hold of the company's technology.

- Price is a sensitive area. It is not uncommon for one partner to find out that they are being underpaid.

- However much the local partner is scrutinised, issues with its governance and ethics could compromise the foreign partner.

- The joint venture is bound to operate differently from the company's home business or a fully owned subsidiary. Management styles might not be compatible. Cultural clashes can also cause serious problems.

- The local justice system and regulators may well favour the local partner in a dispute. And the rules may be stacked against the company to start with. In India, once a joint venture is formed, a company cannot invest in a different one unless its first partner approves – which means it can either veto the move, or extract a high price for its approval.

But with good management, thorough due diligence and watertight agreements, the risks can be minimised. Here are a few rules:

- Don't do it unless the fit is right. The partner company should "share the same vision and values, and be committed to the long term, not in it for a quick buck," says a senior executive at a chemicals company with experience of joint ventures in Russia. Agree on expectations and plans.
- Do thorough due diligence, and structure the agreement to cover as many contingencies as possible. Make sure it is legally enforceable – looking at local precedents may help.
- Make sure that there is someone with joint-venture experience to manage it.
- Think about the exit strategy. Joint-venture agreements can be difficult to withdraw from when they have outlived their usefulness.

It is common to start with a joint venture and move later to a wholly owned subsidiary. BASF, one of the world's largest chemical companies, for example, was legally obliged to enter a joint venture when it entered China in the late 1980s, although it usually prefers to have complete control of its foreign operations. As legal conditions in China have evolved, BASF has steadily bought out its partners and is now largely in full control.

Acquisitions

There are a number of situations where an acquisition will be the best option. For companies coming late to a fairly mature market, this may be the only realistic way to get serious market share. Getting hold of an established brand can be useful if the company's own products are not well-known in a country. An acquisition may also be a way of shutting out competitors.

For retail chains, for instance, acquisition – buying a complete business including outlets, experienced staff, distribution, suppliers and customer base – is a good way to enter new markets. When Walmart wanted to buy its way into the Africa market in 2011, it paid $1.8 billion for Massmart, a retailer based in South Africa with a network of 288 stores across 14 countries in sub-Saharan Africa that it had built up over two decades. By contrast, Walmart had to abandon plans to enter Russia in the same year because it could not secure a suitable acquisition (it is not the only retailer to face this problem in Russia).

Careful research and due diligence are of course crucial. Is a purchase more cost-effective than other modes of entry? Will expensive restructuring be required? Acquisition targets in emerging markets typically need at least some and often a lot of restructuring. And what can be expected to drive the company's revenue growth in the future? This is more significant than its past performance.

Research can take a long time, so a company should carefully assess how long it has got. There is tough competition for the best targets in the leading emerging markets. A local presence focused on the acquisition can help considerably in getting a good picture while developing relationships and moving things along.

Brownfield

Extensive restructuring may make an acquisition in effect a brownfield investment, so-called because the transformation of the emerging-market firm is so far-reaching as to be similar to a greenfield investment. The acquired firm is often completely reformed in such cases, with new staff, systems, technology and products provided by the parent company. Sometimes a brownfield investment is undertaken in order to get hold of an established operation in a highly regulated industry, such as banking or telecoms.

Greenfield

Growth is invariably slower in a greenfield investment. Advantages are that a company has a blank template and complete control, and can focus entirely on building up the business, rather than managing relationships with a partner. This may also be the only realistic option if it needs to protect sensitive intellectual property – which can be the case for manufacturing companies. It may be that the company bases its offer on high quality standards that could not be guaranteed without a fully owned subsidiary, or that its margins are simply too low to allow for another model.

Appointed distributors

An approach that avoids committing too many resources is to appoint a distributor or agency. This may be useful in smaller markets where a large presence is not feasible. Even so, it is still best to have a local presence to advise on sales and marketing and ensure that the company has some control. As discussed in Chapter 8, it is crucial to select a distributor carefully.

This is how Goodyear, a tyre-maker, enters new markets as the first step in a four-stage process. First, it appoints a distributor. Second, it opens a local office to provide leadership, planning, sales support, marketing and training for the distributor. Third, it sets up Goodyear House, a company-owned subsidiary to replace the distributor and take care of all aspects of the business except manufacturing. Fourth, it will set up production, if the market is sufficiently large, in which case the new facility will become a regional production hub. But Goodyear is prepared to be flexible. If it is sure that the market is worth it, it will go straight to stage three, as it did when it entered China in 1988.

Franchises

Franchises, which are popular with restaurant and hotel chains, allow the use of a company's brand in exchange for a share of profits. This is a way to enter a market while keeping financial risk and management resources to a minimum. Again, this may be particularly useful in small markets. Or it may be used in larger markets to penetrate beyond major centres. Adidas, a multinational sports-clothing and accessories designer and manufacturer, has both franchises and own-run stores in Turkey, for example. The key is to have strict controls in place to make sure that the use of the brand is correct.

The legal framework must be sufficiently sophisticated to support the franchise agreement. When KFC, a US fast-food restaurant chain, was looking to enter China in 1987, it decided the legal framework was too weak for it to use the same franchising model as in the US. So it set up joint ventures with state-owned companies, which provided important contacts.

Growth goals

Companies need a clear plan, from an early stage, of how they expect the market to grow. An important consideration is how much of the market to pursue in the initial stages. Expanding into the whole of India or China in just two or three years is almost impossible. Companies need to see where the best potential for their business is – possibly in just one or two leading cities – and build up their market share in those places before undertaking further expansion. Both China and India are best viewed as a collection of small markets.

Establishing the initial foothold will allow a company to get to know how the market operates and decide what works best for the business. In Russia, some firms start to expand beyond Moscow and St Petersburg in a big way only after spending years in the country. In small markets, or if there are already good nationwide distribution systems, it may be possible to penetrate beyond the main cities much more quickly.

It is important to balance promoting the merits of a particular market with maintaining realistic expectations. Coca-Cola opened its first bottling plant in China in 1927. After the communist takeover it was forced out of the country, along with other foreign firms, but it re-entered in 1979. Although it has been growing steadily ever since, it has been consistently profitable only since 1990 – and it is still investing heavily to support its growth.

This demonstrates a crucial point for business strategy in any large emerging market: think long term. It is possible that investments in emerging markets will yield profits sooner than forecast, but more often this phase takes longer than expected as unexpected obstacles arise. So while pitching an ambitious expansion plan to justify large-scale investment, it is important not to oversell the potential returns.

It is also important not to pull out at the first sign of trouble. Companies need to build foundations for their business, invest in relationships and build a reputation – all of which can be destroyed if they pull out when there are bumps and volatility. And it can be hard to come back.

Taking the longer view of an emerging market involves more than just what resources should be deployed. As the final chapter of this section argues, taking a longer-term view of all emerging markets may require a company to restructure its operations globally, and even rethink the very way it does business, if it is to make the most of the new growth opportunities in the world.

10 Rebalancing and transformation

LEADING MULTINATIONALS NOW ACCEPT that emerging markets are likely to account for the majority of their sales. But for most the shift in focus is still very much a work in progress. Emerging markets already account for over half the sales of Nokia, ABB and Unilever, and around one-third of Nestlé's and Procter & Gamble's. But for slower-moving companies the proportion is much lower, just 15–16% for AstraZeneca and Air Liquide, for instance. McKinsey found that in 2010, 100 of the world's largest companies with headquarters in developed economies earned just 17% of their revenue from emerging markets, even though those markets made up 36% of global GDP (and rising).

Companies are moving fast – but not fast enough. For Western firms, the share of global revenues coming from emerging Asia is rising at a staggering speed. According to surveys by the Economist Corporate Network in Asia, Western firms said that Asia (including Japan) contributed 19% of their global revenue in 2011; in 2012 that figures rose to 22%. Firms expect Asia's contribution to be 32% by 2017 – but that would still be below Asia's share of global GDP at 35%. In 2012, 44% of executives at Western firms thought they were underinvesting in Asia relative to the region's opportunity.

Why are companies not rebalancing more quickly? In some cases it is because of a lack of vision, but in many cases it is because building a presence in emerging markets is tough – and becoming tougher. Companies recognise that they need to conquer emerging markets, but find it challenging – for the reasons discussed in the previous chapter.

The new neglect

Multinationals may be swiftly tilting their growth strategies towards emerging markets, and looking for their operations in Africa, Latin America and elsewhere to sustain global growth. But despite the opportunities that growth markets offer global firms, they are often unable to find the capital, talent and other resources they need, and are constrained by the still-cautious outlook that overshadows decision-making emanating from the post-crisis "rich world".

There are two primary challenges for global businesses in their efforts to allocate the appropriate time and capital for their growth markets. First, most multinational companies still formulate business strategies from headquarters based in slow-to-no-growth mature markets, which can limit the ability of emerging-market business heads to secure sufficient funds to build new distribution channels, or design market-specific variants on the company's global products and services. Second, tightened belts in the home market can create internal struggles for management time, staff and cash within various emerging-market businesses, further slowing them down.

Business leaders in charge of growth markets have long bemoaned the lack of headquarters attention to their regions. This was traditionally thought to be because revenues from developing-world markets are relatively small, but the risks are high. But since the 2008–09 financial crisis, this neglect is more nuanced. "I presented a growth plan which was modest and achievable, and in line with headquarters' revenue expectations," says the Asia-based head of global growth markets for a US insurance firm. He was told that the board would not invest in new markets until domestic sales stabilised.

Economic problems in the home market can easily dampen a company's enthusiasm for investment and expansion in the emerging world. The Asia-based emerging-markets CEO of a European telecoms provider says that, despite the surety of its growth model, "it is still very difficult to capture and maintain the attention of the board" in the current unsure global economic environment. With developed economies' struggles hitting the bottom line, the pressure is on to cut costs. And it typically takes time to become profitable in emerging markets. The need to placate shareholders without compromising longer-term success is an extremely difficult balance to strike.

Corporate transformation

The big shift to emerging markets has implications for how companies operate that go far beyond a simple rebalancing of operations. Companies are being forced to rethink where they locate their most senior executives, their global management structure, their organisational structure, and even their corporate culture.

For example, in 2007 John Chambers, CEO of Cisco, a multinational designer and manufacturer of networking equipment, announced that the company was opening Globalisation Centre East in Bangalore, India. He sent one of Cisco's most senior executives, Wim Elfrink, to run the centre, with the title of chief globalisation officer. Elfrink was the first executive to report to Chambers from outside California. The Globalisation Centre East has become Cisco's second headquarters. It houses managers from every function in the company, including sales and marketing, R&D, finance and human resources. Cisco has already moved around 20% of its top management to India. Staff based at Globalisation Centre East sit on all the company's boards, and have a lead role globally in developing new products and services.

Cisco hopes eventually to set up several other similar centres around the world, and it will continue to redistribute senior managers and decision-making rights. The idea is that each region should have equal weight, rather than being seen as subsidiaries of US headquarters. The company aims to build a polycentric approach to its entire business, with its operations clustered in locations that match the emerging power centres of the world.

In an interview with Knowledge@Wharton in 2009, Elfrink explained the impact of the company's presence in India on its products and priorities:

> We recently launched an initiative out of the Globalisation Centre called Smart+Connected Communities. This initiative is focused on working with cities to help them use technology to drive social, economic and environmental sustainability. When I worked in the US, this was priority number ten. Working here, because I live in the

heart of globalisation and demographic shifts, this is now my number one priority. And we have driven it to become a top company priority.

Key principles

While one aspect of the change involves relocating key decision-makers, another involves altering management structures to ensure a proper focus on growth markets. The exact solution will vary by business, but there are three key principles to keep in mind.

Toe dipping is not enough: companies have to get local

As emphasised earlier, a proper understanding of local conditions is essential for success in emerging markets. And to be able to compete in emerging countries, companies need to become as local as possible. To some extent, companies will be able to employ familiar growth strategies in emerging markets, as the development of consumer markets in the emerging world will reflect trends already seen in the developed world. Consumers will become more demanding, and segments will consolidate.

But companies will not be able to just farm out models developed with Western consumers in mind. Product development will increasingly have to focus on catering for the needs of Asian and other emerging-market consumers as a first priority. By 2020, for example, China will match the US as the world's largest consumer market, and around 40% of global car sales will be in Asia. Companies will require a deep understanding of local conditions in order to refine their product offerings correctly and develop innovations, build an effective route to market and respond to rapid changes in the market place. A local presence is crucial.

Decentralise decision-making: empower local operations

A local presence also means some degree of local control. Empowering those who understand the local conditions and opportunities is arguably the key to success. In India, for example, Tata Sky, a direct broadcast satellite television provider, has a national office to handle overall strategy, with other decision-making decentralised to local branches across 25 states. Harit Nagpal, Tata Sky's CEO, says:

You cannot press the execution button from one central office in Bombay for all the policies for the 20 or more regions you may have in the country.

Move with agility: be fast and light

The window of opportunity in emerging markets is a small one. As already argued, competition is strengthening. And first-movers are rewarded – McKinsey noted in a 2012 report that in 17 major product categories in the US, the market leader in 1925 remained the number one or number two for the rest of the century. So companies need to move fast. And because they have to adopt different approaches depending on the country, product type and brand, because they have to respond to variability in growth, and because they need to compete with lower-cost local competitors, they need to be light – a heavy, bureaucratic set-up will not work in emerging markets.

This will also help to address a major issue that Western companies struggle with in emerging markets: profitable growth. Gaining market share is one thing; doing so profitably is another. In an EIU survey of senior executives at multinationals in 2010, just 35% said that their company's investment in Asia over the past decade had led to increased profitability.

Relocating: more big boots on the ground

One aspect of companies' organisational rebalancing is relocating key decision-makers. Part of the reason for the failure of many companies to fully exploit the opportunities in emerging markets is that senior management teams back in European or US headquarters are too distant. They may view the world too much through the prism of their low-growth home markets and fail to fully appreciate the opportunities elsewhere. And even if they do appreciate them, managers based in developed economies may not fully understand how to exploit them.

To combat this, more and more Western firms are moving senior decision-makers to where the growth is. Schneider Electric, a multinational electrical equipment company, and KPMG, a professional services company, both have their global heads based in

Hong Kong. GE and IBM have their global "growth markets" heads in Hong Kong and Shanghai respectively.

The shift is happening at an accelerating pace. In 2008, just 19% of Western companies surveyed by the Economist Corporate Network (ECN) had a member of their main board of directors living and working in the region; by 2012 that figure had risen to 38%. A similar pattern can be seen with other types of senior roles. In 2011, 46% of non-Asian companies said that they had a global business unit head living and working in Asia; by 2012 that had risen to 52%, and 68% of companies expected it to be the case by 2017.

Regrouping: new geographical organisation

Companies are increasingly moving away from traditional regional units (for example, central and eastern Europe or CEE). The Asia CEO of a global telecoms firm told the ECN that his firm's Asian momentum was strong ("we've got no market that's not growing over 15%") thanks to the region's density of high-growth markets full of firms hungry for bandwidth and managed services. That density had brokered an expansion of his turf: "I'm now also in charge of Africa, the Middle East and Turkey." In some cases strategic resources are being pushed up to larger regional units, for example Emerging Europe, the Middle East and Africa (EEMEA). A growing number of multinationals are also dismantling geographically defined boundaries of their management structures in favour of ones organised by GDP growth rates.

These trends sit alongside a third: the formation of overall "global growth markets" units. GE, GlaxoSmithKline and IBM, for example, have reorganised their businesses to have all their growth markets worldwide managed by a single CEO (located in Hong Kong, Singapore and Shanghai, respectively).

With this dedicated focus not only can the sensitivities and requirements of customers in those markets be better understood, but a better perspective can be gained on the relative weighting of each of those growth markets for the business. By joining up emerging markets, and presenting those joined-up opportunities to headquarters, the hope is that board-level awareness can be gained. Synergies between growth regions can also be better exploited: many global firms are seeing increasing potential in the trade between emerging regions. For example, trade between Africa and China alone has grown tenfold in the past decade, to over $200 billion in 2012.

Small country clusters

Support resources, such as HR and finance, are allocated to smaller sub-regional clusters. Sales resources are assigned to countries, or even cities or regions within countries, in order to get as local as possible. The goal is to combine a local presence and decentralised decision-making on local issues on the one hand with strategic flexibility on the other. Clustering countries allows support resources to be close enough to the ground without duplicating functions in all countries (especially important where the countries are small).

Large strategic units

The question then is where should the clusters report to. Companies are finding it best if they report to a large unit. This allows companies to save on costs and increase efficiency at a time of pressure on resources by not having too many layers of management. But it also means they can be more flexible in identifying and responding to rapidly changing growth opportunities; technology and better availability of data mean that the central strategic operation can have a good view of the sub-regional level without needing a regional team in between.

This helps to contain the volatility of emerging markets – rather like hedging a portfolio – and allows for successful forecasting of results. For example, one EEMEA CEO had ambitious growth plans in Egypt before the country's revolution. To compensate for the dip in his results following the upheaval, he was able to reallocate resources to squeeze extra growth from Saudi Arabia, as well as cutting some costs elsewhere. He did not even have to explain the impact of Egypt's problems to global headquarters; it just saw that the overall regional result was all right and was satisfied. The ideal, then, is to have a structure that is large enough to contain volatility without becoming unwieldy.

All this seems to work best if the "growth markets" level is fairly light and predominantly strategic – if it is too top-heavy, it can end up constraining flexibility. IBM made it work. Its Shanghai unit, for example, was responsible for the idea of opening offices in many second-tier cities in large countries. This stresses the point that it is not just a case of grouping the right markets together; it is also about understanding the underlying principles of what you are doing and making sure they are respected.

A more flexible geographical organisation also often meshes better with the fact that many multinationals have complex structures with a number of different business lines. For example, Akzo Nobel, a multinational conglomerate, has 11 business units, ranging from decorative paints to pulp and performance chemicals. The country manager (if there is one) may be limited to an administrative and facilitative role, with key decisions being taken by business units.

Organising around cities

Companies are also starting to consider how to organise to better target cities. This is especially the case in the BRIC economies, where second- and third-tier cities, beyond the largest metropolises, are increasingly the key to growth. Exploding urbanisation in China and India is often highlighted, but even Russia has 14 cities with populations of close to 1m or over, a similar number to the whole of Western Europe.

This may mean further decentralisation of decision-making to strengthen the role of regional organisations in those countries – in most companies they are still mainly just sales functions – which of course fits with the principle of becoming as local as possible. India, for example, with 29 major languages and diverse cultures, often needs a tailored approach for every region. This does not necessarily mean abandoning country structures, as they may be best placed to take a strategic view of city opportunities. Companies may, for example, have regional structures in China based on clusters of cities, while in Russia a possible solution is to divide up the country's vast and poorly connected expanse into several regional blocs, each with a stand-alone manager.

Management hubs

As a growing number of companies are moving senior management functions to emerging markets, and choosing to cluster strategic functions for efficiency and effectiveness, management hubs are emerging. Such centres will have excellent flight connections, good financial services, good availability of top-quality office space, supportive regulations for basing expatriate staff, decent infrastructure and services – and also be pleasant and secure places to be based. Leading hubs include Singapore and Hong Kong in Asia and Istanbul and Dubai in Europe, the Middle East and Africa (EMEA).

The problem is that the leading hubs are now burning up. Companies in Singapore, Hong Kong and Istanbul in particular are struggling with soaring property prices, rising cost of living, tough competition for talent and scarce school places. A CEO at a fast-moving consumer goods multinational in Istanbul lamented:

> We just hired a sales director, and his package is quite close to mine. And when we got a new account manager he cost 50% more than his predecessor.

Cost is the main concern. In an ECN Asia survey in 2013 some 52% of companies with a regional headquarters in Singapore said inflation and the cost of living there were major issues or even possible causes for relocation. Such cost pressures of course reflect demand. It will remain vitally important to have a concentration of management in places that meet all the conditions companies require from management hubs. Hence certain cities will probably retain a pre-eminence for such a role.

But pressures in leading hubs are starting to prompt some firms to consider moving their regional management teams away from these traditional hubs, or at least to move parts of their operations that do not need to be in their regional hubs to less expensive cities in other countries. And some firms are looking at new organisational structures altogether, with more distributed management models that spread their senior team across several markets.

Emerging Asia

In Asia, Singapore and Hong Kong have emerged as the leading hubs, reflecting in part that they have excellent infrastructure by regional standards and are essentially "first-world" cities embedded in an emerging region. Shanghai is rising strongly, reflecting China's weight, but faces similar issues to Hong Kong and Singapore. Other options include Kuala Lumpur and Bangkok.

Emerging EMEA

Istanbul has emerged as a popular choice as a hub for the whole of emerging EMEA, in part reflecting the fact that Turkey is now a top global growth market. Its strategic location, Mediterranean climate and the reach of its national airline also help. Dubai has successfully positioned itself as the normal location for managing the Middle East, although it is facing competition from Istanbul for that role. Moscow retains a role as a management hub for the Commonwealth of Independent States (CIS), but rarely anything wider. Warsaw is increasingly emerging as the leading hub for central and eastern Europe.

Johannesburg used to be viewed as the natural hub for the whole of Africa, in addition to its role as the hub for southern Africa. It retains that position for many companies. But there are alternatives: Nairobi for East Africa (or even for Africa as a whole) and Lagos for West Africa (or alternatively Accra or Dakar).

Latin America

In Latin America, the choice of a hub will typically depend on whether Brazil or Mexico plays the greatest role for a company. In Brazil, São Paulo is the most likely hub, although companies where relations with the government are crucial may choose Brasilia instead. In Mexico, Monterrey used to be a typical choice, especially for US companies given its proximity to the border. But rising crime and the deteriorating security situation there mean that Mexico City is now becoming a popular location. Miami, Santiago and Bogotá are other possible options.

Footloose

Management hubs will remain important for the foreseeable future, but rising cost pressures will see many companies explore variations on the theme. Still, companies are more footloose than in the past, and are relocating their management functions with greater frequency – one-third of respondents to an ECN Asia survey considered this to be the case. This mainly reflects the pace of change in the global economy. A senior executive at a health-care company, commenting on his company's choice of Istanbul as its EMEA management hub, noted that the headquarters had been near Paris for over 30 years but he considered it unlikely that it would be in Istanbul for much more than a decade. The pace of globalisation and localisation meant that before too long it would be necessary to revisit the location again or find a different structure.

Rethinking: an emerging-market mindset

What is ultimately required is a change in mindset as well as a change in organisation. The profound differences in operating in rapidly changing emerging markets and in the developed world mean that companies are increasingly finding that they need to have essentially two separate management teams with a parallel structure for emerging markets. If they do not, either developed markets or emerging markets are likely to be mismanaged. Hence GlaxoSmithKline and Unilever have a global emerging-markets headquarters in Singapore, while Cisco has one in Bangalore.

The emerging-markets team will need to have a very different mindset from the developed-world team. Developed-world companies are proud of their corporate identity, believing that an idea of "who we are'" underlies their success in their traditional markets. But more and more, such firms are realising that having just one corporate identity and mindset does not necessarily work. West European companies, for example, can be relatively risk-averse. But is that ideal for the rapid scaling-up that success in emerging markets may demand? Setting up a new structure for emerging markets allows companies to think about which bits of their corporate identity they want to keep when they operate there, and which they can jettison.

This is the approach that Honeywell followed with its strategy of "becoming the Chinese competitor". Shane Tedjarati says:

> Creating the same spirit of an entrepreneurial Chinese company inside a large multinational company is both an art and a science. We've figured out the science of it and now we're working on the art of it: how to make it part of our culture ... How to make our company more nimble, how to make us more efficient in decision-making, how to bring our product costs and quality and speed to

market in line with what the locals can do, and do better than them. In the areas where we've done this in earnest, we're actually much better than our local competitors.

Conclusion

The shift to emerging markets means huge changes for the way a business operates. A change of mindset is required for Western companies. It is not enough just to be a Western company that operates in emerging markets, using the same models and strategies as in the home markets. Instead, companies need to become truly globalised and think of emerging economies as "home markets" as they do the US or western Europe.

PART 2

Regional and country profiles

The BRICs

Overview

The economic success of the heavy hitters of the emerging world, Brazil, Russia, India and China – known collectively as the BRICs – since the turn of the century – has triggered unprecedented change in the global economy. Most obviously, their rise has accelerated the shift in the global economic centre of gravity away from the struggling developed world to these and other high-growth markets. China has led the way, overtaking Japan in 2011 to become the world's second largest economy and setting itself on course to overtake the US for the top spot in the early 2020s.

As impressive, however, has been the societal transformation of these countries. The reduction in poverty has been extraordinary. China again has led the way, with 500m–600m people being lifted out of poverty since the country was opened to reforms in the late 1970s. In Russia, the share of those in poverty fell from 34% of the population in 1992 to just 14% in 2007–08, and in Brazil since 2003 some 50m people have moved into the middle or upper class.

But just as the BRICs rode the global boom before 2008, so the prolonged post-bubble adjustment that has followed is forcing these four countries to recalibrate their growth assumptions. With around 44% of the global population, the BRICs will remain large, attractive markets for businesses for the foreseeable future. But how far each country is able to reform will determine whether they remain in the vanguard of global growth or are relegated to the second league. So far the signs are mixed. Long-standing internal structural impediments that had been masked by the easy wins of rapid global growth are increasingly re-emerging.

In Brazil, for example, enormous commodity wealth coupled with a lack of competitiveness – in some sectors it is more expensive to run a factory in Brazil than in Germany – has made the country vulnerable to an overreliance on its natural resources to the detriment of manufacturing, a condition commonly known as "Dutch disease". Related to this, one of the legacies of economic volatility is a dearth of investment, which at just under 20% of GDP is below that of Jamaica. An improved business environment and lower interest rates (high rates are a legacy of the hyperinflation of the 1980s–90s) would do wonders for investment and boost long-term growth.

Russia has a similar problem with underinvestment, but unlike Brazil has done little to foster a high-value-added industrial base. Thus growth remains vulnerable to shifts in commodity prices. Notwithstanding high levels of spending on research and development, levels of innovation and entrepreneurship are low, reflecting the poor business climate. Structural bottlenecks also help to keep inflation high. Annual growth projections to 2018 average just below 4%, a better performance than in western Europe, but well down on the 8% notched up in 2003–07.

India, the least developed of the BRICs, has arguably undergone the most abrupt about-turn in its fortunes. During the boom years it was seen as the successor to China as the star member of the group, but political sclerosis, rampant corruption and an inability to get to grips with outstanding macroeconomic problems, such as inflation and the current-account and fiscal deficits, have taken the shine off the India story. Despite having the most favourable demographic profile among the BRICs and huge scope for catch-up in terms of infrastructure improvements, talk now is of whether India will return to its sluggish "Hindu rate of growth", which prevailed before the 1991 reform year.

China remains the cornerstone of the BRIC economies. The 12th and latest five-year plan (2011–15) was notable in seeking to rebalance growth away from a reliance on exports towards domestic demand. But significant challenges remain, not least how to take potentially destabilising economic decisions at the same time as a new political leadership, which took office in late 2012, seeks to entrench its authority. An issue to watch will be whether the government can wean the economy off its dependence on investment to drive growth – at around 50% of GDP this is unsustainably high, even for an emerging market.

The BRICs journey has, therefore, reached a crossroads. Encouragingly for the global economy, the long-term structural story of these countries is unchanged. Brazil, Russia, India and China will all remain markets that are too big for business to ignore over the coming decades. (One by-product of this will be the emergence of the BRICs as fully fledged outbound investors, which will further transform the global economy.) But the easy growth is now past. The achievement of long-term sustainable growth for all four will depend on the ability of policymakers to reform internally rather than look to the outside world for expansion.

CHINA

Historical snapshot

China was traditionally one of the world's largest and richest agrarian economies. However, dynastic decline and a failure to modernise sapped economic and political stability, and in the past two centuries China was scarred by poverty, invasion, civil war and extremes of economic experimentation. Following the communist victory in 1949, the first three decades of Maoist rule were characterised by the radical collectivisation of agriculture and industry and the adoption of Soviet-style central planning. After Mao Zedong's death in 1976, Deng Xiaoping initiated an "open door" policy of decollectivisation and opening up to the global economy, culminating in China's admission to the World Trade Organisation (WTO) in 2001. This brought spectacular economic advances. Still, a legacy of statist policy directives remains a hallmark of China's growth model.

Market dynamics

China's state-owned sector retains a crucial role in national economic development. State-owned enterprises (SOEs) continue to monopolise strategically important sectors (such as heavy industry, energy, financial services, transport and telecommunications). With easy access to credit and political support, the SOEs have grown into massive conglomerates. China's private sector employs more workers, but it is fragmented and mainly operates in light industry and services.

China has continued the Soviet tradition of central economic planning, and the 12th Five Year Plan – a mixture of economic directives and social goals – began in 2010. Monetary policy is government directed. China has a long-term objective to open its capital account and allow the yuan to float freely, but the schedule remains vague. The country's foreign-exchange reserves, at over $3 trillion, are the largest in the world.

GDP was $8.4 trillion in 2012, making China the world's second largest economy (displacing Japan). With a population of over 1.33 billion it has an enormous domestic market, and individual Chinese provinces are sizeable markets in their own right (for example, Sichuan province's GDP is equal to Malaysia's).

An initial post-reform growth spurt was driven by low-cost labour and export-oriented investment policies that made China the "workshop of the world". But things are changing. Three decades after economic reforms began, demographic changes – thanks to the one-child policy – are shrinking the labour supply, while land, utilities and currency costs have risen. In response, the authorities are promoting capital-intensive and high-tech industries.

China remains a highly dynamic economy. However, growth is slowing and major changes are under way. Exports, formerly the main driver of growth, now contribute less than one percentage point to GDP growth, in part the result of export manufacturers relocating to countries with lower costs.

Investment, particularly state-funded investment in fixed assets, has fuelled much of China's recent growth. This has resulted in modern transport and logistics networks linking the main production and distribution centres and providing easier access to inland markets. Better transport and productivity have helped compensate for additional costs. The clarity of China's industrial planning also resonates with investors, and the country remains one of the world's leading destinations for foreign direct investment.

China's policymakers responded quickly to the global financial crisis in 2008 with an enormous two-year stimulus package. This boosted the domestic economy but also inflated asset bubbles, particularly in the domestic property market. Policy measures were introduced in 2011 to curb the property market, which remains fragile. Meanwhile, associated sectors such as steel and construction materials are also weak, as are local-government revenues, which relied on land sales. Indeed, market conditions for most sectors in 2012–13 were anaemic by Chinese standards, but policymakers are resisting another major stimulus package.

The 12th Five Year Plan calls for 13% annual rises in minimum income levels, far outpacing inflation. As a result of such measures, household incomes have risen (per-head urban incomes reached Rmb21,810 in 2011), and although savings rates are still high (at over 50%), domestic consumption is also rising. China's "middle-class" households represent a massive business opportunity that has attracted most global retail chains. Sales within China's markets now account for a growing percentage of global sales for many multinational corporations. H&M, a Swedish multinational clothing retailer, entered the country in 2007. It opened its 100th store, in the fourth-tier city of Nanning, in 2012.

Since joining the WTO, China has initiated new free-trade agreements with major trading partners, such as the China–Taiwan and China–ASEAN trade agreements in 2010. Nonetheless, protectionist tensions are expected to increase, partly because of the growing strength of China's domestic companies as well as in retaliation for perceived discrimination against Chinese commercial actions, or as spillovers from bilateral political disputes. Trade litigation on the part of and against Chinese companies has increased, with most complaints centred on non-tariff barriers, illegal subsidies, anti-dumping and intellectual property rights violations.

China's global investment ties are expected to increase. Its overseas mergers and acquisitions (M&A) activities have diversified from energy resources into manufacturing, financial services, public utilities, agribusiness and retail. Investment destinations are varied, ranging from mines in Africa and Australia to Greek luxury goods (Folli Follie jewellery, watches and fashion accessories). Chery, a Chinese carmaker, for example, is expanding its overseas production to Brazil, while Bosideng, a Chinese clothing retailer, has launched a stand-alone store in London's West End.

Chinese outbound investment has come from state-run sovereign wealth funds, SOEs, private corporations and family-run businesses, but government support and soft loans have given an impression of a government-mandated investment drive. China's M&A activities have at times provoked controversy abroad, and the country has in turn tightened its own foreign investment and anti-monopoly regulations.

Doing business

Businesses must cope with a less compliant and more expensive labour force for their China operations. The labour force is expected to start contracting by around 2015. Although China does not have independent trade unions, collective bargaining and labour litigation are increasing and strikes have become more common.

The government is pursuing a policy of "indigenous innovation" and intends to spend 2.5% of GDP on research and development by 2020. This, and a long-standing policy requiring technology transfers as a condition of some Sino-foreign joint-venture investments, is likely to result in breakthroughs in seven new priority industries (new-generation IT, energy saving and environmental protection, alternative energy, biotechnology, high-end equipment manufacturing, advanced materials and new-energy cars). However, the ability of Chinese firms to innovate in the absence of strong intellectual property rights is questionable.

There is also an emphasis on advanced professional services, particularly in the financial sector – the authorities aim to develop Shanghai as a "global financial centre" by 2020. But financial reforms seem to be running behind schedule.

The rural economy is long overdue for reforms. Household registration and land tenancy practices require modernisation to encourage agribusiness investment and bolster food safety and security. Rural incomes lag far behind urban ones, and although government subsidies and income transfers have increased, the income gap is widening.

Demographic challenges are fast overwhelming government resources to construct a social-security net to cope with the ageing population. Demographic and social change is also being felt in the growth of social media. With 500m internet subscribers and near-saturation rates of mobile phone usage, China has astonishingly rapid communication, adroitly outpacing government censorship efforts. Government corruption is an increasingly frequent target of criticism on samizdat blogs, and is viewed by many as endemic.

Demographic changes and higher income levels are also expected to generate political changes in China. GDP per head is likely to reach $10,000 in 2016, a level of societal development that international experience suggests foreshadows political reform.

TABLE 2.1 **China: economic indicators**

	2005	2006	2007	2008	2009	2010	2011	2012
GDP growth (% real change per year)	11.3	12.7	14.2	9.6	9.2	10.4	9.3	7.8
Nominal GDP[a] (US$bn)	2,287.2	2,793.2	3,504.4	4,547.2	5,105.5	5,949.8	7,314.4	8,358.5
Exports of goods & services (% of GDP)	36.6	38.0	38.3	34.8	26.1	27.7	27.3	25.9
Imports of goods & services (% of GDP)	31.1	30.5	29.5	27.1	21.8	23.9	24.7	23.2
Exchange rate Rmb:US$ (average)	8.2	8.0	7.6	6.9	6.8	6.8	6.5	6.3
Consumer price inflation (% per year, average)	1.8	1.7	4.8	5.9	-0.7	3.2	5.5	2.6
Population (m)	1,276	1,283	1,290	1,297	1,305	1,313	1,321	1,329
GDP per head[b] (US$ at PPP)	4,260	4,930	5,760	6,410	7,030	7,810	8,660	9,450
Inward foreign direct investment (FDI) (US$bn)	104.1	124.1	156.2	171.5	114.2	273.0	331.6	307.9

a Real GDP (gross domestic product) is adjusted for price changes. Nominal GDP includes price effects.
b GDP per head (US$ at PPP; purchasing power parity) is calculated based on an adjustment of exchange rates to reflect differences in the cost of goods and services between countries.
Source: The Economist Intelligence Unit

INDIA

Historical snapshot

British rule in India came to an end in 1947, and Jawaharlal Nehru's government set up a complex system of socialist economic controls that remained largely in place until the 1980s. As a result, the country's economic performance was weak, struggling to grow above 4% annually, despite a rapidly increasing population. It was not until 1991, when India experienced a balance-of-payments crisis, that significant reforms were introduced and the country opened up to international trade and investment. Today, India maintains many vestiges of its socialist, closed-off, bureaucratic past. However, the reforms unveiled in 1991 provided enough freedom for economic growth to rise sharply.

Market dynamics

India is a parliamentary federal democracy – by far the world's largest – with an independent judiciary. But while the electoral process runs smoothly, politics is anything but harmonious. Two main parties dominate national-level politics, the Indian National Congress (set up by Nehru) and the Bharatiya Janata Party (BJP). In recent years, neither has managed to gain a majority, and as the power of smaller regional and caste-based parties has risen, so coalitions have become more unwieldy. Coalition politics is likely to continue.

Under such circumstances, successive governments have found it increasingly hard to get things done. India desperately needs economic liberalisation. Because of the lack of progress, growth has slowed, from 10.5% in 2010/11 (India's reporting year begins on April 1st) to 3.3% in 2012/13. Growth is expected to return to around 6% from 2013/14, but an economy at India's early development stage should be growing much faster.

India remains a relatively poor country. Per-head GDP in 2012 stood at around $1,500, less than one-third of China's level. The vast majority of the population, around 70%, still lives in the countryside. Some 60% of the population is employed in farming, yet agriculture makes up only 17% of the economy. India's cities are the engines of economic growth, and a middle class is emerging that is large in absolute numbers, even if it remains a small fraction of the overall population. The number of people in India's cities is rising sharply, although the government estimates that urbanisation will reach only 36% in 2025, compared with 30% in 2012 (partly because of higher birth rates in rural areas).

With almost one in five of the world's people, a young and rapidly expanding population, and medium-term growth likely to average around 6–7% a year, interest from foreign companies is strong. Many businesses have done exceedingly well, such as Unilever, an Anglo-Dutch consumer goods company, and LG, a South Korean electronics manufacturer.

Companies focus initially on the tier 1 cities, such as Delhi and the surrounding National Capital Region, Mumbai, Bangalore, Hyderabad and Chennai. These are home to India's burgeoning middle class. More established firms are pushing into tier 2 and tier 3 cities, where growth is also strong and penetration of goods and services far lower. Opportunities exist in the countryside too, but they are much harder to exploit and incomes are much lower.

But India is not just an exciting market. Many firms are tapping into its large pool of well-educated engineers. IBM, a multinational technology and consulting company, and Accenture, a multinational management consulting and technology-services company, have vast workforces in India writing software and running business services for global clients. At first these companies were attracted by India's lower wages. However, incomes have risen sharply in recent years, and now the rationale is more about gaining access to deep pools of highly talented workers who are well-versed in outsourcing and IT.

India's large IT and business-services sector is competitive and global in outlook. NASSCOM, an IT trade association, says the industry recorded revenues of $88 billion in 2011, equivalent to 7.1% of India's GDP. Of this, $59 billion came from exports. Western IT companies such as Yahoo! and Symantec now have product-development teams in India that take the global lead in managing certain product lines. India has developed an expertise in "frugal engineering", developing new products that suit the lower incomes of emerging-market customers.

The industrial sector is still relatively underdeveloped, accounting for just 20% of GDP, which is low by Asian standards. With 10m people entering the workforce every year, manufacturing is needed to help with job creation. But this demands major reforms, especially in freeing up the labour market, encouraging investment in infrastructure and attracting foreign investors.

India is hugely diverse. Any company hoping to do business there must recognise the large variations among states in terms of growth rates, income levels, cultural characteristics, government effectiveness and so on. High-growth private-sector industries are concentrated around Mumbai in Maharashtra, in parts of Gujarat, around Delhi, including in Haryana and western Uttar Pradesh, and in the corridor from Bangalore in Karnataka to Chennai in Tamil Nadu. These states account for around 80% of foreign direct investment (FDI).

Doing business

India remains a difficult place for foreign firms to operate in. One of the greatest challenges is massive underinvestment in infrastructure. The huge blackout in July 2012 during which more than 620m Indians lost access to electricity for 24 hours is symptomatic of the lack of investment in energy. This is also evident in the poor state of roads, airports, ports and much other infrastructure. In 2011 investment was below 30% of GDP, too low to provide the infrastructure needed to support high growth rates.

Another macro-level problem is inflation. In part this is a result of underinvestment, which means a lack of economic capacity. As soon as growth picks up, inflation breaks out. In addition, India has highly inefficient agricultural supply chains – yet food makes up a significant part of most people's spending. If a monsoon fails, inflation spikes. Generous government welfare programmes for the poor also drive up prices. The central bank is forced to keep interest rates high, which discourages borrowing and dampens investment.

A third macro problem is the persistent current-account deficit. India imports more than it exports. A big part of its import bill is made up of oil – the country produces little of its own. To balance its payments, India has relied on inflows of portfolio capital – which tend to be short-term and volatile – rather than FDI. This has caused sharp devaluations of the rupee, and the currency is volatile.

TABLE 2.2 **India: economic indicators**

	2005	2006	2007	2008	2009	2010	2011	2012
GDP growth (% real change per year)	9.2	9.3	9.8	4.0	8.3	10.5	6.4	3.3
Nominal GDP[a] (US$bn)	832.8	947.6	1,236.7	1,224.2	1,361.5	1,706.4	1,869.8	1,839.3
Exports of goods & services (% of GDP)	19.3	21.1	20.5	23.7	20.1	21.9	23.9	23.8
Imports of goods & services (% of GDP)	22.1	24.3	24.5	28.6	25.5	26.4	30.4	31.6
Exchange rate Rs:US$ (average)	44.1	45.3	41.3	43.5	48.4	45.7	46.7	53.4
Consumer price inflation (% per year, average)	4.2	6.2	6.5	7.8	11.7	12.1	9.6	9.7
Population (m)	1,094	1,112	1,130	1,148	1,166	1,184	1,202	1,220
GDP per head[b] (US$ at PPP)	2,299	2,550	2,836	2,968	3,193	3,520	3,770	3,900
Inward foreign direct investment (FDI) (US$bn)	7.6	20.3	25.5	43.4	35.6	26.5	34.2	24.0

a Real GDP (gross domestic product) is adjusted for price changes. Nominal GDP includes price effects.
b GDP per head (US$ at PPP; purchasing power parity) is calculated based on an adjustment of exchange rates to reflect differences in the cost of goods and services between countries.
Source: The Economist Intelligence Unit

At a micro level, companies struggle with issues common to many emerging markets. Corruption is ever-present. Tax judgments can be highly arbitrary and uncertain. The regulatory environment lacks transparency and is sometimes contradictory. Labour laws are rigid and draconian.

Land is difficult to buy and purchases are fraught with danger. Local politicians often whip up anger by suggesting the prices companies pay to farmers for their fields are too low. Indeed, opportunistic politicians stirring up nationalist sentiment against foreign companies can be a major impediment generally. Posco, a South Korean steel company, has been trying for years to get an iron-ore mine, processing facilities and port set up in Orissa, but has failed to overcome local opposition. Even Indian companies fall foul of this. Tata Motors, one of India's biggest auto companies, was forced to scrap plans to build a new car factory in West Bengal in 2008 when local politicians turned its land acquisition programme into a political battleground.

More generally, bureaucracy remains challenging, and barriers to foreign investment in many sectors remain entrenched. It can also be challenging finding enough workers with the required skills and experience. While India has huge pools of exceptional talent, the demand for such workers often outstrips the supply.

There are many positive aspects to doing business in India in the medium term, but companies will face many challenges.

BRAZIL

Historical snapshot

Brazil's resilience during the 2008–09 global financial crisis and subsequent rebound instilled a sense of triumphalism in the government of President Luiz Inácio Lula da Silva and his followers. After decades of economic underperformance and hyperinflation in the 1980s and 1990s (a period which saw Brazil's transition to democracy), when it seemed Brazil would forever remain the "country of the future", Lula presided over a GDP growth spurt (averaging 4.5% annually in 2004–10) and the country seemed finally poised to realise its potential. Elected in 2003, Lula consolidated the sound macroeconomic policy framework set up by his predecessor. He reaped a stability "dividend" and also enjoyed the good fortune of a commodity super-cycle driven by insatiable Chinese demand for Brazil's commodities. Rises in the minimum wage and poverty alleviation programmes lifted large swathes of the poor into the lower middle classes – creating a new consumer market.

Fuelling the feel-good factor, large deposits of oil were discovered in 2007 in deep offshore fields that promise to turn Brazil into a top-ten oil producer by the 2020s. And the country won the mandate to hold the 2014 World Cup and 2016 Summer Olympics in Rio de Janeiro – although mass protests over poor social services in 2013 suggested many Brazilians have other priorities. Brazil overtook the UK to become the world's sixth largest economy in 2011.

Market dynamics

Brazil's 2011–12 slowdown – partly triggered by policy tightening to rein in overheating – has had a sobering effect. It is forcing policymakers under the government of Dilma Rousseff (of Lula's leftist Partido dos Trabalhadores, PT or Workers' Party) to address some of problems still holding the country back. The 2013 protests will add to the impetus for reform.

The response has been a mix of stimulus measures and protectionism, neither of which will resolve competitiveness problems. More encouragingly, there is an ambitious plan to upgrade

Brazil's rickety logistics infrastructure by offering concessions to the private sector, rather than persisting with public-sector programmes that have failed to deliver tangible improvements. But more needs to be done to reduce the so-called "custo Brasil", the additional cost of doing business in Brazil. This includes a heavy tax burden, up from 15% of GDP 20 years ago to over 35% of GDP in 2013, red tape and labour-market rigidities. These factors have contributed to keeping the investment rate under 20% of GDP, which is too low.

While portfolio investors have been reducing their exposure to Brazil, multinational companies are keeping the faith. Brazil is an upper-middle-income country with a population of 195m, and the large consumer market is clearly a draw. Foreign direct investment inflows in the 12 months to September 2012 amounted to $64 billion. This is still considerably less than inflows into China, but it puts Brazil well ahead of the rest of the emerging-market pack. As well as market opportunities, foreign companies are on the lookout for opportunities to boost efficiency. For example, in 2012 UnitedHealthcare, a big US health-care company, acquired Amil, a leading Brazilian health-care company.

From a macroeconomic perspective, annual GDP growth of 4% is feasible in the medium term, assuming that government measures to boost competitiveness pay off. This will be weaker than in Brazil's 2004–10 growth spurt, because of slower labour-force growth and a tighter labour market, weaker Chinese growth and slower credit growth. But private consumption growth will still be robust. Loans to households and businesses have doubled to 51% of GDP since 2003, but there is still room for growth, including in mortgages, which were virtually non-existent in 2008 but in 2012 accounted for nearly 6% of GDP. Demand for Brazil's commodities will drive exports, although significant exports of oil will not materialise until the second half of the 2010s.

Doing business

Gradual changes in the macroeconomic policy framework that have occurred since mid-2011 will become more evident to companies operating in Brazil in the medium term. Inflation targeting has become more flexible, allowing central bank interest rates to fall to historically low levels (by Brazil's standards), and the floating-exchange-rate regime has been increasingly heavily managed. There is a risk that interest-rate cuts might have to be reversed if inflation picks up. But lower interest rates should provide the government with some budgetary wriggle-room, even though the public debt to GDP ratio is still high by emerging-market standards (55% in gross terms).

The government has adopted measures aimed at removing infrastructure bottlenecks. In August 2012 it announced an ambitious plan of public–private partnerships (PPPs) in transport and logistics, with ports and airports to follow. It also intends to cut energy tariffs, and reduce the tax burden on certain manufacturing sectors by replacing payroll contributions with a turnover tax.

Although turning to PPPs to upgrade infrastructure shows President Rousseff's pragmatic streak, she is also a moderate interventionist – as can be seen in the energy sector. The plan of Petróleo Brasileiro (Petrobras, the state-controlled oil company) to double local crude production by 2020 (from 2.1m barrels/day in 2012) is being used for industrial policy goals, with high local-content rules for the supply of equipment to lift oil reserves – although this is leading to delays and higher costs. Petrobras's ambitious plans to build local refineries have, however, been scaled back. Nevertheless, there is still scope for more private-sector involvement in energy. New oil concessions were offered in May 2013, after a five-year break.

Meanwhile, the Banco Nacional de Desenvolvimento Econômico e Social (BNDES, the state development bank) will continue to play an important role in industrial policy through its heavy investment lending at low, subsidised interest rates. BNDES, which celebrated its 60th birthday in June 2012, has long supported government development strategies and industrial policies. It has contributed to the creation of "national champions" and supported Brazilian multinationals' expansion abroad. Total loans more than tripled, from just under $20 billion in 2002 to over $72 billion in 2012. But the bank is often criticised for the distortions it creates in the economy. Instead of complementing the private financial sector by lending to companies with little access to credit (such as small and medium-sized

TABLE 2.3 **Brazil: economic indicators**

	2005	2006	2007	2008	2009	2010	2011	2012
GDP growth (% real change per year)	3.2	3.9	6.1	5.2	−0.3	7.6	2.7	0.9
Nominal GDP[a] (US$bn)	881.8	1,088.9	1,366.3	1,652.8	1,621.7	2,141.9	2,473.5	2,252.4
Exports of goods & services (% of GDP)	15.1	14.4	13.4	13.7	11.0	10.9	11.9	12.6
Imports of goods & services (% of GDP)	11.5	11.5	11.8	13.5	11.1	11.9	12.6	14.0
Exchange rate R:US$ (average)	2.4	2.2	1.9	1.8	2.0	1.8	1.7	2.0
Consumer price inflation (% per year, average)	6.9	4.2	3.6	5.7	4.9	5.0	6.6	5.4
Population (m)	180	182	185	187	189	191	193	195
GDP per head[b] (US$ at PPP)	8,793	9,330	10,060	10,700	10,640	11,470	11,900	12,100
Inward foreign direct investment (FDI) (US$bn)	15.5	19.4	44.6	50.7	31.5	53.3	71.5	65.3

a Real GDP (gross domestic product) is adjusted for price changes. Nominal GDP includes price effects.
b GDP per head (US$ at PPP; purchasing power parity) is calculated based on an adjustment of exchange rates to reflect differences in the cost of goods and services between countries.
Source: The Economist Intelligence Unit

enterprises and innovative start-ups), it predominantly lends to large companies.

One area of concern for companies is Brazil's creeping protectionism. For example, in 2012 the government announced new regulations, Inovar-Auto, to encourage innovation in the domestic automotive industry, which is dominated by foreign companies that came to Brazil during an earlier phase of import-substituting industrialisation, operating behind high tariff walls. The programme seeks to boost research and development in modern and environmentally sound vehicles. Incentives include a substantial tax rebate. Critics, however, see the new measures as the latest in a series of protectionist steps, including a 30-point rise in the tax rate on imports of cars.

For this and other reasons, excitement about Brazil has dimmed somewhat since the heady days of 2010, when it was being hailed as the next great investment opportunity. Nevertheless, market potential is huge and it seems likely that enough will be done for Brazil to remain a top growth market for companies.

RUSSIA

Historical snapshot

The Soviet legacy continues to shape Russia's business environment, particularly the structure of its economy and its infrastructure. The country's transition to a market economy under Boris Yeltsin's presidency (1991–2000) was traumatic. Economic "shock-therapy" carried a huge social cost, the business environment was lawless and violent, and the privatisation programme produced a few powerful oligarchs who controlled the country's principal assets. Western companies nevertheless rushed in to take advantage of Russia's rapid economic transition, but suffered when in the country's 1998 crisis the rouble was devalued by 75%, the government defaulted on its debt and the economy crashed.

Vladimir Putin, a former KGB officer who replaced Yeltsin as president in 2000, reasserted the power of the state, and a period of rapidly rising oil prices led to growing prosperity. Russians initially accepted the erosion of democracy, which was associated with the chaos of the Yeltsin years. However, the new middle class began to resent the growing dominance of a single, authoritarian leader and his inner circle, which has shown little sign of ever relinquishing power and has entrenched corruption throughout the system. The 2008–09 global economic crisis exposed the Russian economy's reliance on high oil prices, and since 2011 the worsening political situation has triggered protests.

Market dynamics

Russia's main attraction for many international businesses – and the basis of its inclusion in the BRIC group – is its large, relatively wealthy population (143m, with a GDP per head of $17,600 at purchasing-power parity in 2012). The average is skewed by a high level of inequality, but Russia does have a sizeable middle class. That said, the demographic outlook is poor – the population is forecast to decline to below 140m by 2020, despite the government's pro-birth policies and the health benefits of increasing prosperity.

The economy is dominated by oil and gas, which account for

two-thirds of exports and 40% of budget revenue, and strongly affect growth in many other sectors, including retail. The country also has a sizeable heavy industrial base, especially in metals, chemicals and machinery.

The global economic crisis of 2008–09 hit Russia hard. The economy contracted by 7.8% in 2009, the largest decline among the G20 nations. Growth rebounded quickly, but is unlikely to return to pre-crisis levels. In 2003–07 average real GDP growth was 7.5% annually; in 2012 it dipped to 2.8%; and in 2013–17 the Economist Intelligence Unit (EIU) forecasts that it will average below 4%.

There are a number of reasons to expect slower growth. Energy prices, while remaining high historically, are unlikely to rise as rapidly again as in the years up to 2007 – and the shale gas revolution threatens to bring down prices for Russia's gas exports in the medium term. At the same time, Russia's energy output is likely to stagnate at best. Traditional fields are maturing and inefficient state-owned firms are not investing enough in developing new ones. To prevent declining production, the industry will have to develop more remote and geologically complex areas where the technical challenges and costs are formidable – a point epitomised by the decision in 2012 to abandon plans to develop the Shtokman field in the Arctic.

The government is doing little to improve the efficiency or accountability of state organisations. The conventional wisdom that Russia is well-endowed with human capital looks increasingly out of date, as the education system has deteriorated since the end of communism. The authorities say they want to modernise and diversify the economy, but the difficult business climate deters investment.

Fundamental change to the system is highly unlikely under the current regime. Regulatory improvements and measures such as a new "business ombudsman" are mainly just palliatives. Enough progress is likely to be made to maintain a respectable growth rate, but not to put Russia on a higher growth path. Its entry into the WTO in 2012 is no guarantee of an improvement in the rule of law – and initial signs are that it will do its best to stretch the WTO's rules.

Although economic growth forecasts are well below those of emerging markets in Asia, Russia is wealthier and investors will find it hard to ignore an economy of this size growing at around 4% a year, dependent though this is on high oil prices. The government could bridge a decrease in the oil price in the short term by borrowing, but before long it would have to cut spending.

An economic reversal could trigger further protests that spread beyond the main cities and the middle class. There are also increased tensions within the elite – modernisers were disappointed by Putin's decision to return as president – and these could coalesce with popular discontent to create change. Despite increased repression, the aura of impregnability that used to surround Putin's rule has gone.

Doing business

Notwithstanding Russia's growth opportunities, many companies' regional heads find it a tough sell to global headquarters. Corruption is pervasive. Entering the market and getting things done require patience. Rules are often unclear, local courts are unreliable, and enforcement is patchy. IKEA, a Swedish furniture company, announced in 2011 that it was freezing its Russia plans because of endemic corruption. Finding and retaining talent is also a problem – salaries for senior executives in Russia are high by European standards and rising rapidly.

Russia has a poor image in Western media, not all of it fair. It is a difficult country to understand, and easy to dramatise in ways that do not accurately reflect a much more nuanced reality. The continuation of a cold-war mentality in some quarters does not help. Russia may still be a nuclear power, have a tendency to bully its neighbours and play politics with energy supplies, and it would like to make the former Soviet Union an exclusive zone of influence, but it is clearly no longer an existential threat to the West. Headline stories are apt to dissuade risk-sensitive companies – for example, BP's dispute with its local partner over control of a joint venture, TNK-BP.

However, the openness of the economy varies according to sector. In strategic sectors, which include energy as well as other natural resources, defence and aerospace, the authorities pursue a statist approach and there are tight restrictions on foreign participation. In other sectors barriers to entry are much lower. The government is happy to allow competition and high levels of foreign ownership in areas such as fast-moving consumer goods (FMCG). Hence PepsiCo,

TABLE 2.4 **Russia: economic indicators**

	2005	2006	2007	2008	2009	2010	2011	2012
GDP growth (% real change per year)	6.4	8.2	8.5	5.2	−7.8	4.5	4.3	3.4
Nominal GDP[a] (US$bn)	764.0	989.9	1,299.7	1,660.8	1,222.6	1,524.9	1,899.1	2,029.8
Exports of goods & services (% of GDP)	35.2	33.7	30.2	31.7	28.3	29.5	30.6	29.7
Imports of goods & services (% of GDP)	21.5	21.0	21.5	22.1	20.5	21.1	21.8	22.1
Exchange rate Rb:US$ (average)	28.3	27.2	25.6	24.9	31.7	30.4	29.4	30.8
Consumer price inflation (% per year, average)	12.7	9.7	9.0	14.1	11.6	6.8	8.4	5.1
Population (m)	143	143	142	142	142	143	143	143
GDP per head[b] (US$ at PPP)	11,861	13,288	14,869	16,048	14,917	15,682	16,686	17,590
Inward foreign direct investment (FDI) (US$bn)	15.5	37.6	55.9	74.8	36.6	43.2	55.1	50.7

a Real GDP (gross domestic product) is adjusted for price changes. Nominal GDP includes price effects.
b GDP per head (US$ at PPP; purchasing power parity) is calculated based on an adjustment of exchange rates to reflect differences in the cost of goods and services between countries.
Source: The Economist Intelligence Unit

for example, was able to acquire Wimm Bill Dann, a Russian dairy products and juice producer, for $3.8 billion in 2011.

So is Russia really so bad? Many companies think not. Foreign direct investment is below potential, but still substantial, at $45 billion in 2012 or 2.2% of GDP (although this is partly reinvestment of Russian capital from offshore – Cyprus is Russia's largest source of FDI).

Multinational companies typically enjoy double-digit growth rates. One senior executive from the FMCG sector commented:

We could achieve double-digit growth even if the economy stagnated just by doing what we do better – increasing our number of sales outlets and refining our product offering.

The fact that the difficult business environment puts off some companies means that competition is still lower than in many emerging markets. Moreover, there are plenty of underexploited opportunities beyond Moscow and St Petersburg. Some local administrations support investors, which can make a big difference to the ease of doing business. A prime example is Kaluga, 150km south-west of Moscow, where a young, progressive local government has established the region as an automotive industry hub. Other local governments have started to take note. Companies are pushing ahead with regional expansion plans. IBM, for example, announced a doubling of its network of offices in Russia's regions in 2012.

Russia is a tough place to operate, but as long as the oil price stays high the commercial opportunities will usually be worth the risks involved.

Emerging Asia

Overview

The Asia-Pacific region is vast. It accounts for 35% of the global economy (at purchasing-power parity). It includes the world's second largest (China) and third largest (Japan) economies. The population numbers 3.7 billion people, or 58% of the world total. As these numbers show, Asia's share of the global economy is much less than its share of the global population. But this is changing rapidly. The region is the fastest-growing part of the global economy, and has been for many years.

Asia is rapidly industrialising and urbanising. Within the next few years, China will overtake the US as the world's biggest economy (the EIU predicts this will happen in 2020). Almost all other countries in the region, with the exception of Japan, are also gaining share.

Given Asia's increasing importance in the global economic landscape, multinational companies have high expectations for their businesses in the region. The Economist Corporate Network regularly surveys its 500 client companies in Asia. Those based outside Asia (notably Europe and North America) say that the region accounted for 22% of their global revenues in 2012. By 2017, they expect that share to rise to 32%.

Over recent years, a large driver of growth in the region has been the rise of export-led manufacturing. With the removal of trade barriers and improving IT and communications technology, companies were able to set up factories in Asia and use its large pools of cheap labour to serve customers around the world. Many countries in Asia are much more trade dependent than the global average.

A related force in Asia's growth story has been the globalisation of service industries. Two notable success stories are the rise of IT services in India and the growth of call centres in the Philippines. Asia has thus benefited enormously from globalisation. By plugging their economies into the global system, Asian countries have tapped into global demand and grown on the back of spending from other parts of the world.

Increasingly, however, this picture is changing. The engine of Asia's growth is shifting towards private consumption within the region rather than outside it. As Asia's economies grow, incomes and wages are increasing. Consumer spending is rising swiftly, creating highly attractive markets.

The Asia-Pacific region is often thought of as one large bloc of countries, but it is actually enormously diverse. Indeed, whatever dimension an observer might choose, the region has the full range of possibilities. Be it religion, system of government, economic structure, climate, level of development, financial sophistication, or consumer tastes and preferences, Asia has it all.

Compare two South-East Asian neighbours, Thailand and Vietnam. Thailand is a constitutional monarchy, with regular elections, a dynamic private sector, well-developed banks, sophisticated manufacturing, and GDP per head of $5,070. Across the border is Vietnam, a communist state with a highly centralised economy, inefficient state-owned enterprises that dominate many sectors, weak banks, troubling inflation and GDP per head of $1,380. Both countries are exciting for many reasons, but companies must take heed of the stark differences between them.

The diversity of Asia means that it is difficult to generalise about the opportunities – and the risks – that companies face. But given Asia's high economic growth, and its sheer scale, one thing can be said with some certainty: global multinationals cannot afford to ignore it.

BANGLADESH

Historical snapshot

Bangladesh was established following the war of liberation between West Pakistan and East Pakistan in 1971. Formerly heavily dependent on foreign aid – which accounted for around 85% of the national development budget in 1985 – Bangladesh has transformed its economy since the 1990s.

Market dynamics

Since the end of the most recent period of military rule in December 2008, Bangladesh has enjoyed relative political stability. It has also shown remarkable macroeconomic stability. The economy has continued to grow steadily even when subjected to external shocks, including high global commodity prices. It also demonstrated its resilience during the 2008–09 global downturn, partly because of the still relatively minor role played by exports in the economy – they contribute only around 20% of GDP.

Strong population growth and rapid urbanisation present a host of opportunities as well as challenges. Unlike in many other Asian countries, the working-age population will grow as a percentage of the overall population in the next ten years. In theory this should boost rates of savings, investment and economic growth. However, the government's challenge is to ensure that job creation and provision of education keep up with population growth and urbanisation.

The poverty rate fell from around 60% of the population in 1990 to an average of 31.5% in 2005–10. Despite low average incomes, there is a small but growing middle class, and good opportunities in some service sectors. The telecommunications sector, for example, has experienced rapid growth since deregulation in 1998. With the entry of private-sector operators, mobile penetration has risen from negligible levels to an estimated 56.5% in 2011, according to the International Telecommunications Union (ITU).

Bangladesh has considerable coal and gas reserves, which have attracted a steady inflow of foreign investment in recent years.

TABLE 2.5 **Bangladesh: economic indicators**

	2005	2006	2007	2008	2009	2010	2011	2012
GDP growth (% real change per year)	6.0	6.6	6.4	6.2	5.7	6.1	6.7	6.3
Nominal GDP[a] (US$bn)	60.3	61.9	68.5	79.6	89.4	100.4	111.9	115.6
Exports of goods & services (% of GDP)	16.6	19.0	19.8	20.3	19.4	18.4	22.9	25.0
Imports of goods & services (% of GDP)	23.0	25.2	26.7	28.8	26.6	25.0	31.6	35.3
Exchange rate Tk:US$ (average)	64.3	68.9	68.9	68.6	69.0	69.6	74.2	81.9
Consumer price inflation (% per year, average)	7.0	6.8	9.1	8.9	5.4	8.1	10.7	8.7
Population (m)	141	142	144	146	147	149	151	153
GDP per head[b] (US$ at PPP)	1,164	1,270	1,370	1,470	1,550	1,650	1,780	1,900
Inward foreign direct investment (FDI) (US$bn)	0.8	0.7	0.7	1.0	0.7	0.9	1.1	1.2

a Real GDP (gross domestic product) is adjusted for price changes. Nominal GDP includes price effects.
b GDP per head (US$ at PPP; purchasing power parity) is calculated based on an adjustment of exchange rates to reflect differences in the cost of goods and services between countries.
Source: The Economist Intelligence Unit

However, the exporting of these commodities could generate considerable domestic opposition because of fears that multinational companies are exploiting the country's natural resources at the expense of the local population. The creation of public-private partnerships (PPPs) may go some way towards alleviating these fears. Gas exploration in the Bay of Bengal should intensify following a decision by the International Tribunal for the Law of the Sea (ITLOS) in March 2012 in favour of Bangladesh on maritime borders, which had been disputed by Myanmar. In 2011 the government signed an agreement with Rosatom, a Russian state-owned nuclear company, to construct Bangladesh's first nuclear plant.

Doing business

The main challenges for foreign investors include insufficient infrastructure, energy shortages and a lack of skilled domestic labour. Various initiatives to improve infrastructure are under way, but they are hindered by endemic corruption, which has also led to a cooling of relations with multilateral donors. The government recognises the need to improve the business environment and attract more foreign investment. Business-friendly policies in recent years have included allowing 100% equity ownership by foreign investors and the setting up of export processing zones (EPZs) – areas with superior infrastructure (including better access to power) and lower tax rates.

The private sector has been allowed to flourish, but it remains hampered by patronage and favouritism, which discriminate heavily in favour of incumbents. Competition policy is lacking and trade policy is restrictive by Asian standards. The lucrative textiles industry, the jewel of Bangladesh's manufacturing sector, will remain firmly in domestic hands.

INDONESIA

Historical snapshot

In 1997 Indonesia was as attractive to multinationals as it is today. Despite his authoritarian grip and barely disguised crony capitalism, President Suharto's "New Order" had stewarded an economic expansion exceeding on average 5% per year over more than a quarter of a century in power. Then the Asian financial crisis hit. In 1998 there was economic and political turmoil, resulting in Suharto's resignation. Alongside Indonesia's post-crisis recovery, a thriving participatory democracy swiftly replaced autocratic rule.

Market dynamics

The work done to strengthen economic and political institutions after 1998 gave Indonesia the resilience to withstand subsequent crises. Its recovery from the 2008–09 economic downturn was almost immediate, and it has been one of the world's most stable growing economies since 2000. The EIU expects the $1.2 trillion Indonesian economy to grow at around 6% annually in 2013–17, among the fastest in Asia.

Indonesia is a full participant in globalisation; it depends greatly on exports, particularly of mineral and agricultural resources, and is increasingly dependent on international investment. The country's 4m overseas workers send home over $550m a month.

This global connectivity has kept domestic demand growth robust. Private consumption makes up around 60% of GDP, and it is estimated that over the next ten years, some 75m consumers will enter the middle class. This demand has caused a boom in imports – Unilever's sales of consumer goods in Indonesia grew by over 17% in 2012.

Despite an occasionally ambiguous attitude towards foreign investors, Indonesia is now attracting foreign investment in a range of sectors. Companies are attracted to the country both as a large domestic economy and as a base to export to the rest of South-East Asia. In 2010, for example, Nissan announced plans to centre its regional production of mid-sized, economical family cars in

Indonesia. There has also been significant investment in the apparel, footwear and consumer electronics sectors.

Natural resources is another sector of interest to foreign companies. But the government is seeking to increase its stakes in many of the country's primary mining concessions, in an attempt to increase self-reliance in resource extraction and push the economy up the value chain. Self-sufficiency is a theme in Indonesian development policy, and frequently creates obstacles for foreign businesses; the Ministry of Agriculture has a plan to become self-sufficient in no less than five core staple foodstuffs by 2015.

Indonesia could develop a strong position in more innovative industries. One is alternative energy: the country is reckoned to have the world's third largest supply of geothermal power. Another is mobile communications application development. Indonesia still lacks the core "innovation assets" of other Asian technology tigers like India and China, such as high-quality universities and large numbers of well-educated technology professionals. Yet it does have a unique R&D laboratory of sorts: its young, increasingly affluent and tech-savvy population. Jakarta is reportedly the world's leading city for mobile Facebook usage.

Doing business

Indonesia still struggles to overcome significant obstacles. The government is seeking to "raise the rent", to extract a larger share of the proceeds from international investors, particularly in the natural resource sector and export-oriented manufacturing. For example, new minimum-wage laws will increase base wages by 30–44%. This will bring benefits in pushing Indonesia up the value chain, but it will also put pressure on the economy.

Corruption, lack of infrastructure and opaque regulatory frameworks were the top three reasons foreign multinationals hesitate when considering opportunities in Indonesia, according to the Economist Corporate Network's Asian Business Outlook Survey in 2012.

When added to lingering concerns about security, many multinationals question whether investing in Indonesia is worth the effort. If the government does not keep up the pace on reform, foreign investment could easily take flight.

But there has been some progress. The government's attempts to eradicate corruption stand out. The country is on course to be among the best-performing major economies in the world over the next few years, and it will be hard to ignore.

TABLE 2.6 **Indonesia: economic indicators**

	2005	2006	2007	2008	2009	2010	2011	2012
GDP growth (% real change per year)	5.7	5.5	6.4	6.0	4.6	6.2	6.5	6.2
Nominal GDP[a] (US$bn)	285.9	364.6	432.2	510.2	539.6	709.2	846.3	878.0
Exports of goods & services (% of GDP)	34.1	31.0	29.4	29.8	24.2	24.6	26.3	24.3
Imports of goods & services (% of GDP)	29.9	25.6	25.4	28.8	21.4	22.9	24.9	25.8
Exchange rate Rp:US$ (average)	9,704.7	9,159.3	9,141.0	9,699.0	10,389.9	9,090.4	8,770.4	9,386.6
Consumer price inflation (% per year, average)	10.5	13.1	6.3	9.9	4.8	5.1	5.4	4.3
Population (m)	229	232	235	238	240	243	246	248
GDP per head[b] (US$ at PPP)	3,081	3,310	3,580	3,830	4,000	4,260	4,580	4,900
Inward foreign direct investment (FDI) (US$bn)	8.3	4.9	6.9	9.3	4.9	13.8	19.2	19.6

a Real GDP (gross domestic product) is adjusted for price changes. Nominal GDP includes price effects.
b GDP per head (US$ at PPP; purchasing power parity) is calculated based on an adjustment of exchange rates to reflect differences in the cost of goods and services between countries.
Source: The Economist Intelligence Unit

MALAYSIA

Historical snapshot

Race-based politics has been a defining feature of Malaysia's political landscape since it gained independence in 1957. However, the ethnic mix of its 28m-strong population (53% Muslim Malays, 26% Chinese, 8% Indian and 13% other races) has increasingly become a source of tension, particularly because of policies favouring Bumiputera, the ethnic Malay majority, which have come to be seen as a source of widespread patronage and corruption.

Against this background, the prime minister, Dato' Sri Najib Razak, who took office in 2009, positioned himself as a moderniser. He repealed draconian security laws, reviewed the electoral system and initiated an anti-corruption campaign. In 2010, he launched detailed plans for structural change that aim to attract more investment and shift the economy towards services.

Market dynamics

After many years of high economic expansion, Malaysia has slowed and underperformed relative to the region. A lot of the investment that once flowed into the country has gone to China instead. But rising costs in China may give Malaysia the opportunity to recapture some of this.

Reviving private investment is at the heart of Malaysia's growth plan. There are promising signs that investors are increasingly confident of its prospects – Malaysia received the fifth-highest level of foreign direct investment in Asia in 2011.

Malaysia's open economy is highly exposed to global ups and downs. Some of its exports are commodities, such as oil and palm oil where price is volatile, and a large proportion is electrical goods and components where demand is volatile.

Over the next few years, though, strong domestic demand will propel the country's growth. The EIU expects private consumption to grow by close to 7% annually in 2013–17, driving real GDP growth of over 5% a year.

TABLE 2.7 **Malaysia: economic indicators**

	2005	2006	2007	2008	2009	2010	2011	2012
GDP growth (% real change per year)	5.3	5.6	6.3	4.8	−1.5	7.4	5.1	5.6
Nominal GDP[a] (US$bn)	143.5	162.7	193.6	231.0	202.3	247.5	289.0	304.7
Exports of goods & services (% of GDP)	112.9	112.2	106.2	99.5	91.4	93.3	91.6	87.1
Imports of goods & services (% of GDP)	91.0	90.4	86.3	77.2	71.1	76.3	75.2	75.3
Exchange rate M$:US$ (average)	3.8	3.7	3.4	3.3	3.5	3.2	3.1	3.1
Consumer price inflation (% per year, average)	3.0	3.6	2.0	5.4	0.6	1.7	3.2	1.7
Population (m)	27	27	27	28	28	29	29	29
GDP per head[b] (US$ at PPP)	11,840	12,730	13,740	14,540	14,260	15,140	16,040	17,030
Inward foreign direct investment (FDI) (US$bn)	3.9	7.7	9.1	7.6	0.1	9.2	12.0	10.9

a Real GDP (gross domestic product) is adjusted for price changes. Nominal GDP includes price effects.
b GDP per head (US$ at PPP; purchasing power parity) is calculated based on an adjustment of exchange rates to reflect differences in the cost of goods and services between countries.
Source: The Economist Intelligence Unit

Doing business

Foreign companies have been hampered by long-drawn-out approval processes and a lack of transparency, but the government is now taking steps to create a more competitive, business-friendly environment. It is lightening the regulatory burden, phasing out price controls and subsidies, and introducing incentives, including lower corporate and income-tax rates for selected industries.

Inadequate education and skills levels are also significant

obstacles. Positive discrimination in favour of Bumiputera distorts the labour market and reduces opportunities for other groups – especially ethnic Chinese, the best-educated section of the population – who frequently decide to look for better opportunities abroad. Graduates from Malaysian universities are often of low quality, and complaints about talent shortages and the lack of initiative exhibited by Malay workers are likely to persist.

However, Malaysia has many strengths to build on. It has developed strong manufacturing clusters. Skills from the semiconductor industry in Penang's manufacturing cluster are being successfully redeployed in burgeoning industries such as solar panels – Malaysia is now the world's third largest producer. It is also consistently ranked third in AT Kearney's Global Services Location Index, which assesses the attractiveness of countries globally for outsourcing activities and shared service centres. And it is developing an Islamic finance sector: the central bank has been promoting Kuala Lumpur as a centre of regulation and oversight for Islamic banking and insurance.

PAKISTAN

Historical snapshot

Since independence in 1947 Pakistan has experienced several military coups, and its history has been coloured by political instability as well as conflicts with India. Economic performance has been erratic, with periods of rapid growth interspersed with slumps. The economy was gradually liberalised during the most recent bout of military rule (1999–2008), but civil unrest and the threat of terrorist violence have damaged the business-operating environment since 2008.

Following the September 2001 terrorist attacks in the US, Pakistan became a vital US ally owing to its close proximity to Afghanistan. Its economic fortunes were boosted by large inflows of concessional loans and favourable trading terms. More recently, however, ties with Western partners have become strained, and aid has declined. Growth prospects will remain closely linked to international geopolitics and especially Pakistan's alliance with the US.

Market dynamics

Economic growth is based on the textiles industry, low-end manufacturing and some service sectors. The proportion of the population that is of working age will rise from around 60% in 2011 to more than 67% in 2030. In theory, this presents Pakistan with a "demographic dividend". However, successive administrations have failed to invest enough in social and physical infrastructure, so job creation will be a challenge. Spending on education, at around 2% of GDP, remains low, although there is an increasing emphasis on improving the quality of state education – driven in part by Western concerns over the alleged role of madrassas (religious schools) in the proliferation of Islamic extremism. Still, illiteracy remains a major problem.

Policymaking is generally pro-market. Tariffs have been lowered steadily since Pakistan joined the WTO in 1995, although non-tariff barriers including opaque policymaking, inconsistent regulations and bureaucratic hurdles remain high.

The liberalisation of the power sector in the mid-1990s, under the

TABLE 2.8 **Pakistan: economic indicators**

	2005	2006	2007	2008	2009	2010	2011	2012
GDP growth (% real change per year)	7.7	6.2	4.8	1.7	2.8	1.6	2.8	4.0
Nominal GDP[a] (US$bn)	118.5	137.2	152.4	170.9	167.9	177.2	213.7	224.9
Exports of goods & services (% of GDP)	14.6	14.1	13.2	12.4	12.4	13.5	14.0	12.3
Imports of goods & services (% of GDP)	18.2	21.5	19.8	23.2	19.7	19.4	19.0	20.3
Exchange rate PRs:US$ (average)	59.5	60.3	60.7	70.4	81.7	85.2	86.3	93.4
Consumer price inflation (% per year, average)	9.1	7.9	7.6	19.8	12.1	12.9	11.9	9.7
Population (m)	158	161	164	167	170	173	176	179
GDP per head[b] (US$ at PPP)	2,321	2,497	2,644	2,700	2,750	2,778	2,870	2,980
Inward foreign direct investment (FDI) (US$bn)	2.2	4.3	5.6	5.4	2.3	2.0	1.3	0.9

a Real GDP (gross domestic product) is adjusted for price changes. Nominal GDP includes price effects.
b GDP per head (US$ at PPP; purchasing power parity) is calculated based on an adjustment of exchange rates to reflect differences in the cost of goods and services between countries.
Source: The Economist Intelligence Unit

government of Benazir Bhutto, led to strong foreign investment in the second half of that decade. However, investment then dwindled because of domestic political instability and a bitter dispute between the government's utility, the Water and Development Authority (WAPDA), and Pakistan's largest foreign-backed power project, Hub Power Co, over tariffs. In recent years the government has renewed its focus on attracting foreign investment to alleviate Pakistan's power-supply deficit.

The rapidly growing financial services and telecoms sectors also attract investment. Pakistan's telecoms market is crowded, competitive and ripe for consolidation. As income levels are low, consumer expenditure will continue to be dominated by food. There is a small but growing middle class that will drive consumption of higher-value items, including white goods.

Doing business

The major challenges in Pakistan include low-quality infrastructure, including the transport network and power supply, as a result of decades of underinvestment; a shortage of power; and a lack of skilled domestic labour. The government is seeking to address these problems, but progress is slow. The security situation adds significantly to operating costs. Companies typically have to incur costs to provide security for physical infrastructure, such as telecoms towers and plants, and this is unlikely to change in the near term.

The government is expected to push ahead with a privatisation agenda, which has been stalled since 2006, to shore up the budget. But foreign companies may be deterred by security concerns, particularly given uncertainty about what will follow the withdrawal of international troops from Afghanistan in 2014.

THE PHILIPPINES

Historical snapshot

The 21-year rule of Ferdinand Marcos (1965–86) marked a period of economic decline for the Philippines. In the 1960s it was the second wealthiest country in Asia, after Japan. But economic mismanagement and chronic corruption soon crippled the country's development. A democratic system was re-established in 1986. In 2001, President Estrada was removed in a military-backed civilian coup and replaced by his vice-president, Gloria Macapagal Arroyo, who won the presidential election in 2004. Under her administration the Philippines' economy grew at its quickest pace in decades. But inefficiency and corruption remained major obstacles.

Market dynamics

The current president, Benigno Aquino III, appears committed to rooting out corruption, improving governance and pushing through major reforms. The country seems to be on the right track, with GDP growth of 6.8% in 2012. Government finances are improving, remittance inflows are strong and the export sector is expanding. Reforms to key economic and political institutions are gaining momentum; in 2010–12 the World Economic Forum (WEF) pushed the Philippines up 20 spots in its global competitive rankings.

The resource-rich archipelago certainly holds great promise. The country has some of the richest mineral resources in the world (with an estimated worth of $850 billion), ranking third in the world in gold, fourth in copper and fifth in nickel. But a lack of investment in infrastructure, cumbersome mining laws, conflicts between national and local rules, a strong anti-mining lobby and a bid by the government to increase mining royalties have scared off foreign investors.

The population of 106m presents a huge consumer opportunity, although per-head incomes are still fairly low. It also presents a challenge. The Philippines' labour force is set to grow by more than 50%, from 40.7m workers in 2012 to 61.6m in 2030. This could be a catalyst for sustained economic growth, but it could also lead to an increasing

TABLE 2.9 **The Philippines: economic indicators**

	2005	2006	2007	2008	2009	2010	2011	2012
GDP growth (% real change per year)	4.8	5.2	6.6	4.2	1.1	7.6	3.6	6.8
Nominal GDP[a] (US$bn)	103.1	122.2	149.4	174.2	168.3	199.6	224.1	250.2
Exports of goods & services (% of GDP)	46.1	46.6	43.3	36.9	32.2	34.8	32.0	30.8
Imports of goods & services (% of GDP)	51.7	48.4	43.4	39.4	33.4	36.6	35.6	34.0
Exchange rate P:US$ (average)	55.1	51.3	46.1	44.3	47.7	45.1	43.3	42.2
Consumer price inflation (% per year, average)	7.7	6.3	2.8	9.3	3.2	4.1	4.7	3.1
Population (m)	90	92	94	96	98	100	102	104
GDP per head[b] (US$ at PPP)	2,890	3,070	3,300	3,450	3,450	3,690	3,830	4,080
Inward foreign direct investment (FDI) (US$bn)	1.7	2.7	3.2	1.4	2.7	1.6	1.8	2.8

a Real GDP (gross domestic product) is adjusted for price changes. Nominal GDP includes price effects.
b GDP per head (US$ at PPP; purchasing power parity) is calculated based on an adjustment of exchange rates to reflect differences in the cost of goods and services between countries.
Source: The Economist Intelligence Unit

strain on infrastructure and social amenities, unemployment and social discontent. The Philippines currently struggles with the highest unemployment rate in South-East Asia: 7% in 2012.

Doing business

The driver of prosperity has been the emergence of a strong business process outsourcing (BPO) business. Between 2009 and 2010, the Philippines surpassed India as the global leader in call centres.

However, a lack of English-language proficiency is now holding back the industry. Call centres hire on average only 5% of the applicants they interview, rejecting the others because of their poor English. The poor state of primary education – ranked 98th out of 141 countries in 2012 by the WEF – is a huge obstacle to the emergence of higher-value-added industries and services.

Moreover, the BPO sector provides only about 1% of jobs in the country. For an economy driven primarily by private consumption, job creation and wage growth are crucial. With large numbers of unskilled workers joining the labour force each year, the Philippines needs to develop its manufacturing sector and build up its export industry to soak up the labour supply.

Manufacturing growth has been held back by low public investment in infrastructure. But this is changing – the government plans to spend about $14.3 billion on roads, bridges, ports, power plants and water systems between 2011 and 2016. The outlook for the Philippines – once dismissed as a perennial underperformer – has brightened.

SOUTH KOREA

Historical snapshot

South Korea has developed rapidly since the 1960s through state-led industrialisation. The economy was directed by a series of autocratic presidents until a successful transition to democracy in 1987. Growth has been led by powerful chaebol (industrial conglomerates), some of which, for instance Hyundai, LG and Samsung, have successfully emerged as global brands. South Korea was knocked off course by the Asian crisis in 1997–98, but has since bounced back strongly.

Market dynamics

Although often overshadowed by China and Japan, South Korea is a sizeable economy. It was the world's 15th largest in 2012, with a population of 50m. Following decades of strong economic growth, it is already prosperous, with per-head GDP of over $20,000. The economy looks robust. The fiscal position is strong, public debt is low and there is a sizeable current-account surplus.

Indeed, South Korea is in many respects already a developed economy. What keeps it in the emerging (or perhaps more accurately in this case high-growth) group is that, although growth is slowing as the economy matures, it seems to be defying notions of what is possible for an economy at its stage of development by continuing along a path of strong manufacturing-led expansion. The EIU expects the economy to grow by close to 4% a year in 2014–17.

This is partly because the chaebol have been reformed since the 1998 crisis and have managed to stay competitive. South Korea boasts strong domestic companies in, for example, automotive, shipbuilding, chemicals and electronics. Continued strong growth is being helped by the success of its industrial conglomerates in expanding sales to emerging markets. As with other economies in Asia, South Korea is benefiting from the rise of China.

The country's continued success is also supported by high investment in R&D, and it is developing new high-tech segments such as robotics. More broadly, South Korea's consensus-driven

TABLE 2.10 **South Korea: economic indicators**

	2005	2006	2007	2008	2009	2010	2011	2012
GDP growth (% real change per year)	4.0	5.2	5.1	2.3	0.3	6.3	3.7	2.0
Nominal GDP[a] (US$bn)	844.9	951.8	1,049.2	931.4	834.1	1,014.9	1,114.5	1,129.6
Exports of goods & services (% of GDP)	39.3	39.7	41.9	53.0	49.7	52.3	56.0	56.5
Imports of goods & services (% of GDP)	36.6	38.3	40.4	54.2	46.0	49.7	54.0	53.4
Exchange rate W:US$ (average)	1,024.1	954.8	929.3	1,102.0	1,276.9	1,156.1	1,108.3	1,126.5
Consumer price inflation (% per year, average)	2.7	2.3	2.5	4.7	2.8	2.9	4.0	2.2
Population (m)	48	48	49	49	49	49	50	50
GDP per head[b] (US$ at PPP)	22,782	24,213	26,077	26,658	26,673	28,605	29,799	30,810
Inward foreign direct investment (FDI) (US$bn)	6.3	3.6	1.8	3.3	2.2	1.1	4.8	5.0

a Real GDP (gross domestic product) is adjusted for price changes. Nominal GDP includes price effects.
b GDP per head (US$ at PPP; purchasing power parity) is calculated based on an adjustment of exchange rates to reflect differences in the cost of goods and services between countries.
Source: The Economist Intelligence Unit

but adaptive society is responsive to the challenges of remaining competitive in the global economy.

There are some concerns. That South Korean companies are focused primarily on growth abroad raises some questions about the vibrancy of the domestic economy. The services sector remains underdeveloped. An increase in household debt since 2011 is a worry. And a rapidly ageing population is a challenge for the government.

Doing business

Relations with South Korea's bellicose neighbour to the north are another risk – but also an opportunity. Although the financial cost of reunification when the North Korean regime eventually collapses (as seems likely) would be high, low public debt should allow South Korea to cope, and companies in the country would gain access to North Korea's sizeable and disciplined workforce.

Despite South Korea's economic strength and good track record of growth, foreign direct investment has been low by Asian standards. This partly reflects the difficulty of competing with strong domestic companies, as well as complex and obstructive regulations and negative public sentiment towards foreign ownership. The government has a highly interventionist stance.

Free-trade agreements in recent years with the US and EU, among others, are making the economy more open to imports. Still, although the future for South Korea looks bright, how far foreign businesses will be able to profit from it is questionable. They may find that the country is more a source of competition than a target for investment.

THAILAND

Historical snapshot

Thailand's most recent military coup in 2006 removed the Thai Rak Thai government led by Thaksin Shinawatra. Thaksin is in exile after facing corruption charges, but the Puea Thai Party, led by his younger sister, Yingluck Shinawatra, won the 2011 election. Beneath these changes, the fundamental faultline in Thai politics is the monarchy. The elderly King Bhumibol Adulyadej is revered by many Thais, and Thaksin is seen as a threatening force to those who want to preserve the royalist establishment and protect the crown. King Bhumibol's eventual death will be deeply destabilising. Thailand's stringent lese-majesty law has prevented open debate about his succession, adding to uncertainty. The power struggle that has destabilised Thailand since 2006 is likely to continue.

Market dynamics

Political drama notwithstanding, the economy has performed well since 2000. In recent years, though, it has suffered from a number of external shocks. Thailand is heavily reliant on exports and so subject to the vagaries of the global economy. In addition, devastating floods in 2011 left several large industrial zones under water and the economy suffered badly as a result – growth dipped to just 0.1%. But the economy has recovered strongly, and the EIU expects GDP to show average healthy growth of just below 5% annually in 2013–17.

Thailand has traditionally been an attractive investment destination thanks to cheap labour, flexible labour laws and a favourable regulatory environment. Large FDI inflows have helped it become a leading exporter in sectors including vehicles (particularly light pickup trucks), electronics (notably hard-disk drives) and electrical appliances. And the consumer market is an increasing draw: the population is large (70m), young, and increasingly prosperous (per-head income is close to $10,000 at purchasing-power parity).

TABLE 2.11 **Thailand: economic indicators**

	2005	2006	2007	2008	2009	2010	2011	2012
GDP growth (% real change per year)	4.6	5.1	5.0	2.5	−2.3	7.8	0.1	6.5
Nominal GDP[a] (US$bn)	176.4	207.1	247.0	272.6	263.7	318.9	345.7	366.0
Exports of goods & services (% of GDP)	73.6	73.6	73.4	76.4	68.4	71.3	76.9	75.0
Imports of goods & services (% of GDP)	74.7	70.2	65.0	73.9	57.8	63.9	72.4	73.8
Exchange rate Bt:US$ (average)	40.2	37.9	34.5	33.3	34.3	31.7	30.5	31.1
Consumer price inflation (% per year, average)	4.5	4.6	2.2	5.5	-0.9	3.3	3.8	3.0
Population (m)	65	65	66	66	67	68	68	69
GDP per head[b] (US$ at PPP)	6,838	7,397	7,939	8,242	8,040	8,700	8,810	9,470
Inward foreign direct investment (FDI) (US$bn)	8.1	9.5	11.3	8.5	4.9	9.1	7.8	8.6

a Real GDP (gross domestic product) is adjusted for price changes. Nominal GDP includes price effects.
b GDP per head (US$ at PPP; purchasing power parity) is calculated based on an adjustment of exchange rates to reflect differences in the cost of goods and services between countries.
Source: The Economist Intelligence Unit

Doing business

For Thailand's economy to be attractive over the longer term, the government needs to improve the education system, as well as develop the telecommunications and transport infrastructure, which remains poorer than in China or Malaysia, its rival manufacturing locations. Thailand has failed to capitalise on advances in telecoms technology, despite hosting many advanced telecoms services and high-tech industries. In particular, obstructive bureaucracy has held back the development of 3G mobile services, where Thailand now is behind even Cambodia, Laos and Vietnam. The government has unveiled an ambitious infrastructure-development programme, but it remains to be seen if it will be implemented as outlined.

Labour costs are surging. From January 2013 all workers in Thailand are entitled to a national daily minimum wage of Bt300 (about $10), which means minimum wages in the country have risen by 70% in less than a year. This has hurt Thailand's competitiveness for manufacturing compared with lower-cost locations, such as Bangladesh, Cambodia and Vietnam.

At the same time, Thailand's workforce has relatively poor productivity. Businesses generally find it difficult to hire people with adequate technical skills as well as basic reading and writing skills. Thailand ranked 54th out of 56 countries globally (and the second-lowest in Asia) for English-language proficiency in a 2011 global competitiveness report by IMD, a Swiss business school. Much will depend on whether the country's polarised politics prevents governments from getting to grips with these problems.

VIETNAM

Historical snapshot

Much of Vietnam's recent history has been turbulent. A struggle against French colonial power after the second world war evolved into a mainly US war, and after the US withdrew in 1973 South Vietnam fell to communist forces from the North. At first, the government pursued socialist transformation. But by the 1980s it was clear that such policies were failing, and the Communist Party of Vietnam (CPV) implemented its doi moi (economic renovation) programme in 1986.

Market dynamics

Vietnam has taken major steps towards being more market-oriented, but its economy remains highly controlled by the government, and the CPV retains complete political control. State-owned enterprises (SOEs) account for 40% of GDP, and the government still operates five-year plans.

Over the 26-year period since doi moi, Vietnam's economy has grown by an annual average of 7% in real terms – although the country is still relatively poor on a per-head basis. However, it also faces serious macroeconomic challenges. High inflation has been a persistent problem. The banking system is weak and poorly run. Years of exuberant lending inflated property bubbles in many parts of the country which are now deflating. Economic mismanagement extends to the currency, with frequent devaluations in recent years.

Vietnam attracts foreign investors for many reasons. Some are looking for a production base; others for a fast-growing market. It has rapidly established itself as an alternative to China for low-cost export-based manufacturing, such as shoes, toys and textiles, as Chinese labour costs have risen. At the same time, it is developing a more sophisticated manufacturing sector, especially around electronics. Global manufacturers such as Intel and Foxconn have invested billions of dollars. Vietnam also has some petrochemicals wealth, and is regularly the world's second largest exporter of rice.

As for the domestic market, Vietnam offers a population of 90m, of which 55% are less than 25 years old. Literacy rates are high, and internet penetration far higher than in other countries of a similar income level (in 2012, 45 out of every 100 people were internet users). The population is growing rapidly, adding around 1m people a year, and urbanising. At present 30% of the population lives in towns and cities, but the urban population is rising by close to 1m each year.

While incomes remain relatively low for most of the population, spending power is rising. Between 2012 and 2016 the number of households earning $5,000 or more a year – a recognised threshold for the middle class – will triple from 1.4m to 5.3m. And in financial services, foreign banks have been attracted by the low penetration of bank accounts (only 20% of the population has one) and credit cards.

Many other industries offer exciting opportunities too. Tourism, for example, is attracting lots of investment, with hotels and golf courses being developed along Vietnam's lengthy coastline.

Doing business

As ever in an early-stage emerging market, the big opportunities in Vietnam are matched by big challenges. Of greatest concern is the mismanagement of the economy. Living with inflation that sometimes touches 20% creates problems in managing wages, and labour unrest has grown in recent years. The weak state of the currency is another worry, and at times it is hard to convert dong into dollars.

Corruption is ever-present, especially in the large state-owned sector, which occupies a privileged place in the economy. The authorities cling to SOEs as a means of keeping political control of the economy, which means politically connected but incompetent managers are allowed to build up sprawling empires that make little business sense and saddle the SOEs with enormous debts. The government has been promising to reform its sprawling SOEs for years, but progress has been agonisingly slow.

The country also suffers from a lack of investment in infrastructure. New roads and the like are being built, but they are not keeping pace with Vietnam's growth. Likewise, the regulatory and legal environment is underdeveloped. These challenges are taking some of the shine off Vietnam's position among foreign investors. Nevertheless, the country will continue to offer huge opportunities.

TABLE 2.12 **Vietnam: economic indicators**

	2005	2006	2007	2008	2009	2010	2011	2012
GDP growth (% real change per year)	8.4	8.2	8.5	6.3	5.3	6.8	6.0	5.0
Nominal GDP[a] (US$bn)	53.0	61.0	71.1	90.3	93.2	103.6	122.8	142.6
Exports of goods & services (% of GDP)	69.4	73.6	76.9	77.9	68.3	77.5	87.0	84.2
Imports of goods & services (% of GDP)	73.5	78.2	92.7	93.1	78.7	87.8	91.2	87.1
Exchange rate D:US$ (average)	15,841.8	15,980.5	16,077.9	16,440.4	17,799.6	19,130.5	20,649.0	20,858.9
Consumer price inflation (% per year, average)	8.3	7.4	8.3	23.2	6.9	10.0	18.7	9.1
Population (m)	84	84	85	86	87	89	89	90
GDP per head[b] (US$ at PPP)	2,130	2,360	2,600	2,800	2,950	3,160	3,380	3,580
Inward foreign direct investment (FDI) (US$bn)	2.0	2.4	6.7	9.6	7.6	8.0	7.4	8.4

a Real GDP (gross domestic product) is adjusted for price changes. Nominal GDP includes price effects.
b GDP per head (US$ at PPP; purchasing power parity) is calculated based on an adjustment of exchange rates to reflect differences in the cost of goods and services between countries.
Source: The Economist Intelligence Unit

Emerging Europe

Overview

Emerging Europe's star has waned since the 2008 global financial crisis. It was the emerging region that was hardest-hit by the economic downturn; some economies suffered double-digit contractions in GDP. The crisis raised questions about its growth model being excessively reliant on foreign capital inflows, in the case of central and eastern Europe (CEE), or on oil, in the case of Russia. The boom and bust left some of the region's economies nursing prolonged hangovers. And its proximity and close economic ties to western Europe started to look more of a hindrance than a help once the euro-zone crisis developed.

There is another issue for business. Some of the region's economies are increasingly mature. The wealthiest EU members in CEE, Slovenia and the Czech Republic, have per-head incomes higher than Greece and Portugal's, and the other CEE EU members (with the exception of Romania and Bulgaria) are not far behind. There is still scope for some growth premium over western Europe, but the business landscape already resembles mature markets in many respects. Competition is tough, and it is difficult to gain market share through organic growth. But these wealthier markets are still important for volumes. As the regional CEO of a fast-moving consumer goods company says:

> We won't look to these markets for future growth. We'll focus on reaping the benefits of great margins and then invest that cash in higher-growth markets.

By contrast, countries in south-east Europe (SEE) and, especially, the Commonwealth of Independent States (CIS) are still recognisably emerging markets. Russia and Turkey (for those companies that include it in Europe) stand out as two growth markets of global significance. In these two countries there are still good growth opportunities to be tapped for at least the next ten years – especially in second- and third-tier cites beyond the leading metropolises.

This raises the question of how far it makes sense any more to treat emerging Europe as a single region. Companies increasingly think it does not, and many have been busy reorganising their management structures since the crisis. A growing number, including Dupont, Adidas, Unilever and Philip Morris International, have split off the more mature parts of emerging Europe, usually Poland and the rest of central Europe, plus the Baltic states and Slovenia, and handed them over to western Europe. The rest of the region is then generally divided into various clusters within an emerging EMEA (Europe, the Middle East and Africa) structure.

So emerging Europe is fragmenting. And even within the sub-regions, there are important variations. Although almost all countries are expected to grow more slowly than before the crisis, when growth rates were boosted by unsustainable growth in borrowing, some economies are better placed than others.

The divergence between northern and southern Europe that has become apparent in the euro zone extends into CEE as well. Poland, the Czech Republic and Slovakia have competitive, well-run economies, decent institutions and a good chance of catching up with the richer west European economies. The Baltic states too look well-set, after taking extremely tough measures to recover from spectacular busts.

Hungary, however, has fallen prey to highly polarised politics and seems to be regressing. And SEE's recovery has lagged. The economies of SEE lack the broad, competitive manufacturing bases of countries such as Poland, and domestic demand is suffering the aftermath of pre-crisis credit binges. Bulgaria has managed to achieve economic stability but not to restart growth. Romania is undergoing a difficult restructuring under IMF auspices, but with its 22m population it could yet be a significant growth market for business.

In the CIS, Russia plays an important role in driving its neighbours' economies, but the picture there is also mixed. Ukraine continues to disappoint. With its 50m population and position on the border of the EU, companies often look at it hopefully as the next Poland, but in truth Ukraine's institutions and elite are not up to the task. Belarus, with its well-educated workforce, would be of interest if it ever reformed, but that will require political change.

Multinational companies are starting to take Central Asia and the Caucasus seriously, thanks to strong growth rates and slowly improving (albeit still tough) business environments. Kazakhstan, in particular, is becoming a mainstream market for business; Azerbaijan is also of interest for its oil wealth. Uzbekistan is the area's population heavyweight, but the risks (including expropriation) are high; gas-rich Turkmenistan is slowly opening up.

Overall, there is a sense that the boom times are over for the region, and that a slower-growth future is in prospect. There will be some improvement as the euro zone – still the principal export market for most economies in the region – eventually emerges from its malaise. Investment is supported by the shift towards nearshoring as opposed to offshoring for manufacturing. The region's good skills base also makes it popular for services outsourcing, especially for IT. Combined with the fact that emerging Europe tends to punch above its weight in terms of global sales for multinationals and retains good growth potential in key markets, this will keep the region on the map for global business.

POLAND

Historical snapshot

In June 2012, Poland co-hosted the European football championship with Ukraine. Looking at the bright, prosperous host cities, it was easy to forget that Poland had emerged from communism barely more than two decades earlier. A violent clash between Polish and Russian football fans proved the main reminder of the country's difficult history. Poland's recent past is much more positive. Since the early 1990s, the country has managed a successful transition from communism to a democratic market economy, consolidated by NATO membership in 1999 and EU membership in 2004.

Market dynamics

Poland has emerged as a stand-out market in CEE for business over the past few years. Its economy was previously seen as rather sluggish, hampered by excessive bureaucracy and poor infrastructure. But views changed when it displayed considerable resilience during the 2008–09 crisis – it was the only country in the EU to avoid recession.

Poland's sizeable domestic market (38m population) is pretty healthy. It avoided the worst of the ramp-up in credit before 2008 that led to boom and bust in many countries in CEE, thanks to both a well-run banking sector and a reluctance among households to take on too much debt. Government budgets have been fairly disciplined. Furthermore, EU funding (worth almost 3% of GDP annually in 2007–13) has allowed a massive programme of investment in infrastructure.

Importantly, Poland's politics has also improved. Eccentric populist parties occupied much of the political scene in the early 2000s, culminating in government in 2003–07 by the xenophobic, conspiracy-obsessed Law and Justice (PiS) party. But the 2007 election was won by the sensible, centrist Civic Platform (PO), which gained re-election in 2011. The PO is cautious on reform but is pushing through some important changes, including raising the retirement age.

Poland's success is not guaranteed. Although it has been holding up well in the face of euro-zone weakness, it is clearly not immune,

TABLE 2.13 **Poland: economic indicators**

	2005	2006	2007	2008	2009	2010	2011	2012
GDP growth (% real change per year)	3.6	6.2	6.8	5.0	1.6	3.9	4.5	2.0
Nominal GDP[a] (US$bn)	303.9	341.3	425.0	529.3	430.0	469.2	514.8	489.7
Exports of goods & services (% of GDP)	37.3	40.4	41.0	39.8	39.7	42.3	45.2	46.0
Imports of goods & services (% of GDP)	37.9	42.3	43.7	43.6	39.6	43.6	46.4	45.6
Exchange rate Zl:US$ (average)	3.2	3.1	2.8	2.4	3.1	3.0	3.0	3.3
Consumer price inflation (% per year, average)	2.2	1.2	2.5	4.4	3.8	2.6	4.2	3.7
Population (m)	38	38	38	38	38	38	39	39
GDP per head[b] (US$ at PPP)	13,573	14,879	16,364	17,570	17,990	18,900	20,010	20,780
Inward foreign direct investment (FDI) (US$bn)	11.1	21.5	25.6	15.0	14.4	17.1	15.3	3.0

a Real GDP (gross domestic product) is adjusted for price changes. Nominal GDP includes price effects.
b GDP per head (US$ at PPP; purchasing power parity) is calculated based on an adjustment of exchange rates to reflect differences in the cost of goods and services between countries.
Source: The Economist Intelligence Unit

and growth slowed markedly in 2012–13. In the longer term there is still a danger that Poland's catch-up dynamics could develop into a boom and bust similar to Spain's. But policymakers seem wise to the dangers.

Doing business

Poland is already a fairly mature economy by emerging-market standards, and competition is strong (one factor in this is Poland's broad stratum of competitive small and medium-sized enterprises). Hence, multinational companies are not looking for double-digit growth. But its size and resilience, along with the growth premium it still offers over west European economies, mean that it will continue to hold an important place in companies' EMEA strategies.

As well as the draw of the large internal market, Poland is attractive for more advanced manufacturing, and benefits from a good education system that makes it well-placed to benefit from the outsourcing services, especially in IT, that will be one of the big growth areas for CEE in the coming years. The country seems on course for sustained growth, and has a good chance of catching up with the wealthier nations of western Europe.

TURKEY

Historical snapshot

Business perceptions of Turkey have changed dramatically since the turn of the century. Previously it was something of a misfit, viewed as at best a useful bridge between West and East. Now it has taken centre stage as a leading growth market. This owes much to Turkey's newfound political and economic stability. The evolution of modern Turkish politics has been difficult, with military coups in 1960, 1971, 1980 and 1997. And economic liberalisation from 1983 was followed by frequent boom and bust. But reforms in the aftermath of the country's last financial crisis in 2001 ushered in a period of improved economic stability. Meanwhile, under the generally pragmatic government of the conservative, moderately Islamic Justice and Development Party (AKP) since 2002, democracy has taken deeper root – although the government's heavy-handed response to large-scale protests in 2013 showed worrying signs of regression.

Market dynamics

Turkey is likely to be a top-ten global growth market for the next decade or so. Its economy is strong. First, the demographics are favourable: the population is expected to rise to over 80m by 2020 and is young (half are under 29). Second, indebtedness is low. Public debt was just 38.5% of GDP in 2012, and private debt is also low. Third, the financial system is solid. Turkey's banks have been run cautiously since the financial crisis of 2001. Fourth, economic policy is supportive. The AKP government is pro-business and pro-investment (if sometimes protectionist and unpredictable).

The large consumer market is clearly a major attraction. The population is already relatively prosperous (GDP per head of $15,000 at purchasing-power parity) and inclined to consume. The government has ambitious modernisation programmes, notably in health care and infrastructure, which will be carried out partly through public–private partnerships (PPPs) and build-operate-transfer. In the health-care sector, for example, ten large PPPs worth $10 billion are being rolled out.

Still, there are risks. Turkey runs a large current-account deficit, which leaves the economy vulnerable were capital inflows suddenly to dry up in the event of a European or global financial crisis. The government is trying to address the issue by encouraging more local production. It is also aiming to reduce Turkey's reliance on imported energy by boosting renewables and building nuclear power plants. But these policies will take time to make a difference. On the plus side, Turkey's strong fundamentals mean that even if the economy did experience a sharp stop, it could be expected to bounce back quickly.

Political risks are also significant. There is the decades-old Kurdish issue that obstructs the development of the south east and poses a moderate security risk elsewhere in the country. A peace process has begun but is far from certain to succeed. There is also political polarisation. Protests in 2013 were partly about the government's heavy-handedness, but also reflected concerns about the future of the secular state. And Turkey extends into an unstable part of the world, as fears about spillover from the civil war in Syria highlight.

Doing business

Turkey is a highly competitive market. The major international players will all invariably be present in any sector. There are also typically strong local competitors, typified by large diversified conglomerates such as Koc Holdings and the Sabanci Group.

The business environment is moderately good – lagging behind the EU members in CEE but comparing well with other large emerging markets globally. A major issue for companies is the tax system. Tax evasion is high, which puts international firms at a competitive disadvantage. Another problem is that labour-market regulation is too rigid. The government has said that it will reform both areas, but progress is likely to be slow.

Infrastructure is also an issue, but it has already improved considerably, making the cities in Turkey's vast interior far more accessible. Other major projects now under way mean that transport connections should more than keep pace with the country's economic expansion (although within the cities, notably Istanbul, the picture is less reassuring).

It seems doubtful that Turkey will ever join the EU, but business no longer seems to care – Turkey has market access through its customs union with the EU, and actually joining no longer seems necessary for the its economic development.

Istanbul has already emerged as a leading management hub for EMEA, and companies are increasingly looking at producing there as well. They are also making Turkey a leading and immediate priority as a growth market. "I don't see any issues – just opportunities," says a country manager in the health-care sector. "Companies have four to five years to make it or break it in Turkey."

TABLE 2.14 **Turkey: economic indicators**

	2005	2006	2007	2008	2009	2010	2011	2012
GDP growth (% real change per year)	8.4	6.9	4.7	0.8	−5.2	9.3	8.8	2.2
Nominal GDP[a] (US$bn)	482.3	529.9	646.9	730.4	614.0	730.7	774.4	789.0
Exports of goods & services (% of GDP)	21.9	22.6	22.4	23.9	23.4	21.2	23.9	26.4
Imports of goods & services (% of GDP)	25.4	27.6	27.5	28.3	24.4	26.7	32.6	31.6
Exchange rate TL:US$ (average)	1.3	1.4	1.3	1.3	1.5	1.5	1.7	1.8
Consumer price inflation (% per year, average)	8.2	9.6	8.8	10.4	6.3	8.6	6.5	8.9
Population (m)	70	70	71	72	73	73	74	75
GDP per head[b] (US$ at PPP)	10,710	11,690	12,470	12,710	12,040	13,210	14,540	14,990
Inward foreign direct investment (FDI) (US$bn)	10.0	20.2	22.0	19.8	8.7	9.0	16.0	12.6

a Real GDP (gross domestic product) is adjusted for price changes. Nominal GDP includes price effects.
b GDP per head (US$ at PPP; purchasing power parity) is calculated based on an adjustment of exchange rates to reflect differences in the cost of goods and services between countries.
Source: The Economist Intelligence Unit

UKRAINE

Historical snapshot

Since independence from the Soviet Union in 1991, Ukraine has existed awkwardly between East and West. The Orange revolution in 2004 brought a pro-Western government to power following a contested election and seemed to promise change, but amid infighting in the Orange camp the mood turned sour. In 2010 Viktor Yanukovych, the regime candidate in 2004, defeated Yulia Tymoshenko, a key figure in the Orange revolution, in the presidential election, and started backtracking on democratisation. Tymoshenko was imprisoned on charges that appeared politically motivated.

Market dynamics

Ukraine has long been viewed hopefully by business as "the next Poland" – a country with a large (50m) population on the edge of the EU. But reality has disappointed. Ukraine enjoyed an economic boom from around 2005 as cheap credit from abroad flooded in. But it was one of the hardest-hit countries in the region when the money dried up in the 2008–09 financial crisis. The hryvnia plummeted and the economy crashed, contracting by 15% in 2009. Recovery since then has been feeble, and the country remains highly vulnerable to a new financial crisis. The banking system is still a mess, the government is strapped for cash and the currency is vulnerable to a renewed slide. GDP per head of just $7,600 at purchasing-power parity in 2012 is extremely low by European standards.

The economy remains reliant on heavy industry inherited from the Soviet Union. Steel is a critical export, accounting for 40% of the total. The country's agricultural sector – the former "breadbasket" of the Soviet Union – holds huge potential. But legal issues around land ownership have hampered foreign investment, although it is now increasing. Ukraine also has fairly well-developed retail and service sectors, albeit with vast scope for further expansion.

TABLE 2.15 **Ukraine: economic indicators**

	2005	2006	2007	2008	2009	2010	2011	2012
GDP growth (% real change per year)	2.7	7.3	7.9	2.4	−14.8	4.2	5.2	0.2
Nominal GDP[a] (US$bn)	86.1	107.8	142.7	180.0	117.2	136.4	163.4	176.3
Exports of goods & services (% of GDP)	51.5	46.6	44.8	46.9	46.4	50.7	54.4	50.9
Imports of goods & services (% of GDP)	50.6	49.5	50.6	54.9	48.1	53.7	60.6	59.3
Exchange rate HRN:US$ (average)	5.1	5.1	5.1	5.3	7.8	7.9	8.0	8.0
Consumer price inflation (% per year, average)	13.5	9.1	12.8	25.2	15.9	9.4	8.0	0.6
Population (m)	47	47	47	46	46	46	46	46
GDP per head[b] (US$ at PPP)	5,580	6,230	6,960	7,320	6,330	6,710	7,230	7,390
Inward foreign direct investment (FDI) (US$bn)	7.8	5.6	10.2	10.7	4.8	6.5	7.2	7.8

a Real GDP (gross domestic product) is adjusted for price changes. Nominal GDP includes price effects.
b GDP per head (US$ at PPP; purchasing power parity) is calculated based on an adjustment of exchange rates to reflect differences in the cost of goods and services between countries.
Source: The Economist Intelligence Unit

Doing business

A major weakness is Ukraine's reliance on gas imports from Russia, which has used these as a source of political leverage, raising prices sharply in recent years and turning off the taps twice. The country has large gas reserves of its own, but the poor business climate and lack of government vision mean that foreign companies have been unwilling to invest in their development. A major deal with Shell in 2013 to develop shale gas reserves may presage a change, but it remains to be seen how far the investment will be implemented and whether other energy companies will follow.

Ukraine's real problem is that the oligarchs who dominate the economy and heavily influence the country's politics are resistant to changes that would lessen their grip. Since 2010 the business climate has deteriorated alarmingly under the Yanukovych administration and corruption has worsened. Companies operating in Ukraine have experienced an increase in tax inspections and fines.

A "deep and comprehensive free-trade agreement" with the EU has been negotiated which would do much to bind Ukraine more closely into the European economy and help improve the quality of its institutions. (It is also a way to make up for the fact that the EU is not willing to offer Ukraine a clear prospect of membership.) But signature and ratification are vulnerable to Ukraine's political situation and pressure from Russia.

Ukraine's potential has always been obvious, and it is certainly possible for businesses to do well there. But the risks are high, and for now it is likely to remain a country of potential rather than promise.

Middle East and North Africa

Overview

Business in the Middle East has proved surprisingly resilient in spite of the upheavals of the past few years. Regionally, companies have returned strong levels of growth. Admittedly, many had to contend with temporary disruptions in some markets, such as Egypt, or suspend operations in others, such as Libya and Syria. But companies that have suffered a decline in their regional business have mostly done so on account of exposure to Iran, where tightening sanctions have all but shut down their operations.

However, it will take time for normality to return to the Arab revolutionary states. Until then, the business environment will remain risky and uncertain. Libya and Tunisia are making only halting progress, while Egypt is facing deep political and economic challenges which will take years to play out. Syria will prove an even longer-term problem. Yemen will remain unruly and unstable for many years.

Yet, apart from Egypt, these revolutionary states play a peripheral role in corporate regional portfolios. International companies show little sign of withdrawing from these markets. Most foreign firms in the Middle East and North Africa (MENA) are there for the long term and view the regional turbulence as a short-term hitch to be managed. Experienced multinationals have learnt that customers often reward them for their loyalty, and that having a strong local presence actually helps them manage shocks better. As one executive succinctly put it: "Risk mitigation is about being local."

Companies with a strong local presence have also been able to react swiftly to the opportunities that have arisen. Governments throughout the region have responded to the unrest by spending, especially in the oil-producing markets of the Gulf, supported by high oil prices; already companies are benefiting from a growing number of tenders and a rise in consumer spending.

Young populations and high birth rates are expanding the consumer base, while gradually rising affluence is inflating purchasing power. Consequently, real GDP growth across MENA is expected to remain high.

MENA is attracting more attention than ever from global headquarters. As one senior executive said: "In the four years between 2006 and 2010, I had one visit from a global board member; between 2010 and 2012, I had five." But increased attention brings its own challenges. Where once regional presidents and vice-presidents were given considerable leeway to make their own decisions, now their boards are monitoring their investment strategies more closely. This risks slowing the decision-making process and diminishing local agility.

Many companies are already at an advanced stage of implementation; they have strengthened their local presence in key territories and are preparing their strategies for expansion into tier 2 markets. In many cases, this entails a re-evaluation of stakeholder relationships, in some instances resulting in the severance of long-standing partnerships and the creation of new ones. While the local partner/distributor model still takes precedence throughout the region, companies are looking to make those relationships more efficient and effective.

Foreign firms in MENA will have to carefully monitor shifts in consumer attitudes as well. The regional turmoil was driven by the demand for "bread and dignity" – economic opportunity and political accountability – and it is these dynamics that are likely to shape consumer attitudes in the new Middle East.

The Arab spring has raised expectations. Young Arabs now expect their rulers to be more responsible, more responsive and more transparent. They are likely to expect these same attributes from the brands with which they associate themselves. Certainly, they are now just as likely to stand up to international companies as they are to their governments.

Resourcefulness, creativity and innovation will impel a new spirit of enterprise. Revolutionary fervour has uncovered a deep reservoir of creativity, long suppressed by corrupt bureaucracies and stultifying dictatorships. Brands that break down barriers and offer something different and new will find fertile ground in this new culture.

The gap between the rich and the poor will widen, while at the same time the middle class will grow. Companies will increasingly compete in the middle ground, where the price/quality equation will become more important. Companies that remain wedded to a single segment of the market, in terms of price or product offering, will probably struggle to retain market share in the longer term.

These attitudes will shape employees' mentalities as well. Demands for higher wages are on the rise. Having found their voice, Arabs are now exercising it on the shop floor. Strikes are far more common across the region, and companies will have to spend more time and money on managing employee demands.

Governments are more likely to side with the employee rather than the employer. Indeed, the overriding focus on jobs and stability will probably entail populist policies, focusing on short-term social issues, rather than longer-term competitiveness. This will inevitably mean higher costs for international business.

The United Arab Emirates

Along with Saudi Arabia, the United Arab Emirates (UAE) is the backbone of companies' MENA portfolios, and is also the regional safe haven and business hub. For many companies it is neither an emerging market nor a developed market, but its importance as a regional hub is not in doubt. It is the third largest economy in MENA, after Saudi Arabia and Iran, and despite a small population (just 7.5m), high disposable incomes and increasingly sophisticated spending patterns make it an attractive market for international companies. Its economy is by far the most diversified in the Gulf.

Much of this is attributable to Dubai, which has regained its bounce since the crash of 2009 and boasts an unparalleled combination of infrastructure (both physical and virtual), capital (both human and financial), vision and nerve. The government knows full well that it has to stay ahead of the game if Dubai is to remain competitive, and this pioneering spirit should stand it in good stead for the future.

Abu Dhabi is diversifying, but it remains far behind its more energetic neighbour.

In many respects the UAE is already a developed economy. Its GDP per head of around $55,500 in 2012 is certainly at that level. But its continued rapid development sets it apart and means that it is still in some senses "emerging". There is huge government spending on infrastructure and on economic diversification efforts. Dubai is focusing on the three Ts (trade, tourism and transport), while Abu Dhabi is developing its petrochemicals, pharmaceuticals and metals industries, among others, although it will remain heavily reliant on oil and gas. Meanwhile, despite attempts at "emiratisation", the UAE's economy will remain dependent on immigrant workers; nationals make up only 11% of the population.

ALGERIA

Historical snapshot

Algeria's recent history has been traumatic, with hundreds of thousands of people killed in a brutal civil war in the 1990s between secular security forces and Islamic radicals. Since the generals triumphed, the country has become more prosperous and stable, under the leadership since 1999 of President Abdelaziz Bouteflika. Algeria came through the Arab spring largely unshaken. But its leadership remains wary about renewed instability and is relatively isolationist.

Market dynamics

Algeria is a sleeping giant in business terms. It has a sizeable population (36m) and economy (the fifth largest in MENA) and is also cash rich – it has foreign-exchange reserves of around $200 billion and an oil reserve fund of around $90 billion. At 9% of GDP, its debt is among the lowest in the world. The economy is dominated by oil and gas, which account for 97% of exports and around 75% of government revenue.

Despite its economic potential, Algeria's traditional hostility to foreign interference means that foreign direct investment is limited. Foreign investors can hold only up to 49% of a local business, for example. The economy remains centralised and inefficient, and suffers from overregulation and heavy bureaucracy. Infrastructure is antiquated. Underinvestment means that the country is poor as well; GDP per head is low at around $9,000, and poverty and unemployment are widespread in rural areas.

The government had been spending modestly in a bid to create jobs, improve the provision of housing and utilities, and develop non-hydrocarbons industry and the services sector, but it is now having to rationalise spending amid concerns about future energy revenues. Oil output growth is low, which will keep economic growth sluggish in the near term at least, and a difficult business climate means that development of the non-oil sector will remain limited.

TABLE 2.16 **Algeria: economic indicators**

	2005	2006	2007	2008	2009	2010	2011	2012
GDP growth (% real change per year)	5.1	2.0	3.0	2.4	2.4	3.3	2.5	2.7
Nominal GDP[a] (US$bn)	103.2	117.2	135.2	171.5	137.8	161.8	198.5	212.1
Exports of goods & services (% of GDP)	47.2	48.7	47.0	47.8	35.2	38.3	38.9	36.5
Imports of goods & services (% of GDP)	24.1	21.9	24.8	28.6	35.8	31.3	28.4	28.6
Exchange rate AD:US$ (average)	73.3	72.6	69.3	64.6	72.6	74.4	72.9	77.5
Consumer price inflation (% per year, average)	1.6	2.5	3.5	6.7	5.7	3.9	4.5	8.9
Population (m)	33	34	34	35	35	36	37	38
GDP per head[b] (US$ at PPP)	7,061	7,291	7,569	7,807	7,929	8,136	8,352	8,550
Inward foreign direct investment (FDI) (US$bn)	1.1	1.8	1.7	2.6	2.7	2.3	2.6	1.5

a Real GDP (gross domestic product) is adjusted for price changes. Nominal GDP includes price effects.
b GDP per head (US$ at PPP; purchasing power parity) is calculated based on an adjustment of exchange rates to reflect differences in the cost of goods and services between countries.
Source: The Economist Intelligence Unit

Doing business

Part of the problem is that the military remains hugely influential in the economy. It determines how a large part of the state budget is spent and is said to control up to 15% of the import market. Alongside entrenched state-owned companies that benefit from cheap funding channelled through the banking system, this restricts the development of the private sector, as well as opportunities for foreign companies.

Algeria is unlikely to change significantly until the power of the military and security services is weakened; they have a huge vested interest in the status quo, and will stamp down on any signs of internal dissent, although the public appetite for revolution is limited given Algeria's past instability. Islamic militants remain a threat, and an attack on a gas facility in 2013 will give the government an excuse to retain a strong focus on security.

Political succession to the ageing Bouteflika is looming, but the signs are that it will be well-orchestrated and kept within the establishment. It is, however, hard to know what is going on behind the scenes in Algeria's secretive political system. Without political change, Algeria is likely to remain a frustrating market – one with huge potential, but still in the "too difficult" basket for most companies.

EGYPT

Historical snapshot

Egypt's revolution of January 2011 brought an end to President Hosni Mubarak's 29-year rule. But the country's transition to majority rule progressed only haltingly in the following months and it became quickly apparent that getting rid of the dictator was the easy part. Although the revolution was about "bread and dignity" – economic opportunity and political accountability – two years into the transition, religion had hijacked the agenda. Many Egyptians had become increasingly concerned that that the new Muslim Brotherhood government under President Mohammed Morsi was more interested in consolidating its own power and imposing its ideology, rather than tackling the country's ills. Following popular protests against the government in mid-2013, the army ousted Morsi.

After the coup the army laid out a road map that provided for a short transition period followed by new elections. But it also decided to crack down hard on the Muslim Brotherhood. Hundreds were killed in violence in August. As of mid-2013, the fate of Egypt's revolution hung in the balance. The army's actions and the Brotherhood's response had deepened the rift in society. Egypt appeared at serious risk of descending into a festering civil conflict, as experienced in Algeria in the 1990s, and there were also signs that the army might be presiding over a counter-revolution.

Market dynamics

At 82.5m in 2012, Egypt's population is the largest in the MENA region. However, the size of its economy fails to match its demographic might, standing fourth in the regional rankings behind Saudi Arabia, Iran and the United Arab Emirates. Historically, the services sector, notably tourism and receipts from the Suez Canal, has dominated the economy, making up almost 50% of GDP. The economic heartland of the country centres on greater Cairo, which consumer-focused businesses claim makes up around 50% of the market by itself. But the persistently high levels of unemployment, which have – officially at least – hovered around at 10% for decades, have prompted a brain drain, with much of the country's best talent seeking employment opportunities overseas, particularly in the Gulf. It has also encouraged the growth of a large informal economy, which the Ministry of Finance thinks represents some 30% of total economic activity but may be up to twice the size of the formal economy on some estimates.

Somewhat ironically, in the final years of Mubarak's rule the country experienced its longest and strongest run of economic expansion, with real GDP growth averaging 5.6% annually in the seven years between 2004 and the end of 2010. Structural reform, including the lowering of duties, tariffs and taxes, during that period helped raise disposable income, consumption and investment while simultaneously broadening the tax base. This supported a marked rise in GDP per head, which more than doubled, from $1,034 to $2,539. Nevertheless, this is a comparatively low figure and Egypt remains the second poorest country in MENA, after Yemen.

This relative poverty, lack of economic opportunity (some 700,000 young Egyptians enter the labour market every year with little chance of finding a job) and, in particular, the huge disparities in wealth were some of the underlying causes of the 2011 revolution which eventually toppled Mubarak – and of the ensuing instability.

Doing business

In mid-2013, two years after the revolution, business confidence in Egypt was low. Even before the upheaval that followed the coup, sporadic episodes of violence had seriously curtailed tourist arrivals, and foreign direct investment had plummeted. The pound was under pressure amid a looming balance of payments crisis, and the budget deficit had deteriorated because of increases in public-sector wages, welfare payments and fuel subsidies. A proposed IMF deal remained in abeyance.

Business with the government and local companies was sluggish. Order books were low or even empty, as local companies lacked the hard currency to pay for products and the government continued to defer payments. Production among local producers and suppliers remained well below capacity as they were unable to access hard currency to pay for necessary imported inputs.

TABLE 2.17 **Egypt: economic indicators**

	2005	2006	2007	2008	2009	2010	2011	2012
GDP growth (% real change per year)	4.5	6.8	7.1	7.2	4.7	5.1	1.8	2.2
Nominal GDP[a] (US$bn)	93.2	107.9	132.2	164.8	188.0	214.4	231.0	254.4
Exports of goods & services (% of GDP)	30.3	30.0	30.3	33.0	25.0	21.3	20.6	18.6
Imports of goods & services (% of GDP)	32.6	31.6	34.8	38.6	31.6	26.6	24.7	26.2
Exchange rate E£:US$ (average)	5.8	5.7	5.6	5.4	5.5	5.6	5.9	6.1
Consumer price inflation (% per year, average)	4.9	7.6	9.5	18.3	11.8	11.1	10.1	7.1
Population (m)	72	73	74	76	77	78	79	81
GDP per head[b] (US$ at PPP)	4,644	5,035	5,456	5,875	6,102	6,390	6,530	6,680
Inward foreign direct investment (FDI) (US$bn)	5.4	10.0	11.6	9.5	6.7	6.4	−0.5	2.8

a Real GDP (gross domestic product) is adjusted for price changes. Nominal GDP includes price effects.
b GDP per head (US$ at PPP; purchasing power parity) is calculated based on an adjustment of exchange rates to reflect differences in the cost of goods and services between countries.
Source: The Economist Intelligence Unit

Consumer spending, however, continued to defy all logic. It seems there is plenty of cash in the market thanks to the parallel economy. So consumer-goods companies were enjoying strong growth, based on getting the basics right and maintaining a strong localised presence that provides good visibility.

But the violence that followed the overthrow of Morsi threatened to make things worse. It certainly increased the risks. Most multinational companies had been able to operate fairly normally over the 18 months following the revolution, but as violence spread they were closely monitoring the situation and temporarily closing down operations as necessary.

Whether a semblance of normality will return – and whether the government will be able to fix the economy and encourage investment – will depend on whether the country's politics can be stabilised and prolonged civil strife avoided.

IRAN

Historical snapshot

Since the 1979 revolution overthrew the rule of the pro-Western shah and turned Iran into an Islamic republic, the country has been a pariah. A period of economic liberalisation from the late 1990s to early 2000s proved short-lived and a conservative backlash brought Mahmoud Ahmadinejad to power as president in 2005. A new president, Hassan Rowhani, elected in 2013 is likely to adopt a less confrontational foreign-policy stance, but conservative elements remain highly influential. Tensions with the West and Israel over Iran's nuclear programme, which it maintains is for peaceful purposes, threaten to ignite a regional conflict.

Market dynamics

Iran should offer an enticing opportunity for foreign businesses. Its oil reserves are the fourth largest in the world and it has the second largest gas reserves. Although unarguably dominated by oil and gas, Iran's economy is one of the Middle East's most diversified, with the region's largest automotive sector (and 13th largest in the world by production) and significant construction, chemicals and agriculture industries. A large, young population means Iran could develop a deep consumer base, eager for high-quality imported or foreign products.

However, Iran's economic fortunes are closely linked to its political situation. The dispute between Iran and the West over its nuclear programme is a drag on its economy and hindering investment, both foreign and domestic. After posting real growth rates comfortably over 5% a year from 2001 to 2010, Iran's economy slowed as the threat of military conflict re-emerged and harsher sanctions were imposed by the US and EU. The currency has slumped as the country's access to foreign exchange is crimped by sanctions. And negative real interest rates mean that savings are kept in physical assets such as gold coins or property and not injected into the wider economy.

TABLE 2.18 **Iran: economic indicators**

	2005	2006	2007	2008	2009	2010	2011	2012
GDP growth (% real change per year)	4.7	6.2	6.4	0.6	4.0	5.9	1.7	−3.0
Nominal GDP[a] (US$bn)	204.3	242.5	307.5	356.0	362.7	422.6	435.2	454.0
Exports of goods & services (% of GDP)	33.5	33.2	33.1	30.3	25.8	27.6	28.2	26.1
Imports of goods & services (% of GDP)	24.1	23.8	21.3	22.1	21.2	20.7	20.0	17.2
Exchange rate IR:US$ (average)	8,964.0	9,170.9	9,281.2	9,428.5	9,864.3	10,254.2	10,616.3	12,175.5
Consumer price inflation (% per year, average)	13.4	11.6	17.1	25.5	13.5	10.2	20.6	19.9
Population (m)	70	71	71	72	73	74	75	76
GDP per head[b] (US$ at PPP)	9,821	10,635	11,500	11,682	12,110	12,846	13,200	12,890
Inward foreign direct investment (FDI) (US$bn)	3.1	1.6	2.0	1.9	3.0	3.6	4.2	4.9

a Real GDP (gross domestic product) is adjusted for price changes. Nominal GDP includes price effects.
b GDP per head (US$ at PPP; purchasing power parity) is calculated based on an adjustment of exchange rates to reflect differences in the cost of goods and services between countries.
Source: The Economist Intelligence Unit

Doing business

The conservative political establishment in Iran remains resistant to foreign investment. Officially, the government allows foreign companies to operate, provided they do not exceed 25–35% of the market (depending on the sector). But the operating environment is challenging and subject to political interference, and foreign companies are likely to be used as scapegoats for increased international pressure on Iran.

State enterprises have privileged positions in most sectors and preferential terms for foreign exchange. During Ahmadinejad's presidency, the Islamic Revolutionary Guards Corps, a branch of the armed forces, increased its economic influence. Its engineering arm has taken a large share of government contracts (including in the oil and gas sector). Powerful bazaar merchants – who are resistant to international goods undercutting their products – also influence economic policymaking. Iran is notionally in the process of privatising state enterprises, but shares are often allocated to other government-linked institutions (such as workers' pension funds).

The oil and gas sector is one of the most frustrating for foreign businesses. Significant spending is needed to keep Iran's ageing oil fields producing. The government is investing in the giant South Pars gas field and could develop a liquefied natural gas export capability. International firms can participate in exploration and development contracts (although the constitution forbids foreign ownership in the sector).

However, EU and US sanctions prohibit companies from supporting Iran's hydrocarbons sector because of its significant contribution to government revenue. An EU embargo on imports of Iranian oil and the threat of US sanctions on companies that deal with Iran's central bank, which clears oil payments, have cut into oil production. For all its promise, Iran will present considerable risks for foreign firms until the political situation changes.

IRAQ

Historical snapshot

Since Saddam Hussein's regime was toppled by a US-led invasion in 2003, Iraq has suffered prolonged violence. Although this has lessened from the extreme levels of 2006–07, militia and insurgent groups are still able to perpetrate deadly attacks, and the government remains weak. US troops withdrew in 2011. Sectarian and ethnic faultlines underscore political instability. Shia constitute some 60% of the national population. The rise to prominence of Shia parties since 2003 sits uneasily with many Sunni Arabs, the previous ruling elite. There is also the issue of Iraq's Kurdish population, who could eventually press for secession.

Market dynamics

Iraq is an oil economy. Oil brings in more than 90% of export earnings and government revenue. Iraq is among the world's top five countries for proven oil reserves with some 143 billion barrels. Output is increasing from both newly developed fields in Iraqi Kurdistan and existing fields in the south, where the bulk of production is located. In 2012 exports reached record highs, surpassing 3m barrels a day (b/d), and the government aims to export 6m b/d by 2017. This may prove optimistic, but a strong upward trend is likely and will fuel rapid economic growth.

A large chunk of foreign investment comes from oil companies. This will continue, despite the lack of a national hydrocarbons law and fierce disagreements between the central government and the Kurdistan Regional Government (KRG) over management of the energy sector.

With rising output and high oil prices, the government has money to spend. Substantial investment deals have been agreed in residential housing, defence and security, and to remedy the parlous state of the electricity and water sectors. The telecommunications sector has also attracted interest and there has been increased investment in the banking sector, although on a small scale given its manifold problems. Meanwhile, oil money is filtering down and releasing pent-up demand for consumer goods.

TABLE 2.19 **Iraq: economic indicators**

	2005	2006	2007	2008	2009	2010	2011	2012
GDP growth (% real change per year)	4.4	10.2	1.4	6.6	5.8	5.9	8.2	8.5
Nominal GDP[a] (US$bn)	36.4	54.8	74.9	131.6	111.7	135.5	180.6	206.9
Exports of goods & services (% of GDP)	–	–	–	–	–	–	–	–
Imports of goods & services (% of GDP)	–	–	–	–	–	–	–	–
Exchange rate ID:US$ (average)	1,468.7	1,467.4	1,254.7	1,193.1	1,170.0	1,170.0	1,170.0	1,166.2
Consumer price inflation (% per year, average)	37.0	53.2	32.5	2.9	–2.8	2.4	5.6	6.1
Population (m)	27	28	29	30	31	32	33	33
GDP per head[b] (US$ at PPP)	3,500	3,860	3,920	4,140	4,290	4,470	4,780	5,130
Inward foreign direct investment (FDI) (US$bn)	0.5	0.4	1.0	1.9	1.5	1.4	3.5	3.7

a Real GDP (gross domestic product) is adjusted for price changes. Nominal GDP includes price effects.
b GDP per head (US$ at PPP; purchasing power parity) is calculated based on an adjustment of exchange rates to reflect differences in the cost of goods and services between countries.
Source: The Economist Intelligence Unit

Basra, Baghdad and the Kurdish region are the three main areas for investment. Some 80% of Iraq's exports pass through the Basra oil terminal. The Kurdish region has been attractive to foreign companies because it is more peaceful than the rest of the country and has better infrastructure and services.

GDP growth has strengthened, inflation has come down dramatically since 2007 and the Central Bank of Iraq has managed the exchange rate fairly successfully. In the longer run it remains to be seen whether oil proves a blessing or a curse. The economy produces little else and if energy prices were to drop so would Iraq's prospects, putting further strain on the fragile political balance.

Doing business

The business environment will remain extremely challenging. Security risks and political instability are major concerns for potential investors, as are interrelated problems of widespread corruption, a weak judiciary and a lack of rule of law. The regulatory regime lacks transparency, and the heavily bureaucratic character of the Iraqi state also makes life hard for business. Infrastructure has suffered from wars and decades of underinvestment, and a combination of insecurity and government inefficacy has hindered reconstruction.

Despite these problems and risks, foreign companies are entering the market, stimulated by the prospect of Iraq's bounteous oil resources, the massive investment needed to rebuild the country and enormous growth potential across all sectors.

SAUDI ARABIA

Historical snapshot

Oil remains the lifeblood of the Saudi economy. Despite persistent attempts to wean itself off its reliance on oil, the kingdom's dependency has actually grown. Oil revenues make up around 88% of exports and a similar proportion of budget revenue. The government has channelled significant resources into its diversification efforts. Indeed, since 2000, the size of the non-oil economy has grown threefold. But the rapid rise in the price of oil and a concomitant increase in state spending mean oil dependency has deepened. Consequently, the kingdom remains exposed to the vagaries of the global energy market.

Market dynamics

Saudi Arabia is the second largest economy in MENA after Iran, accounting for 16% of regional GDP in 2012. In recent years, it has also been one of the fastest-growing economies in the region. As such, it is the foundation upon which corporate regional portfolios are built.

Government spending remains the bedrock of growth, underpinning both public and private consumption. In the decade to the end of 2010, it rose almost threefold; by the end of 2015, it will have risen almost by a factor of five. The political turmoil that has rocked the Arab world since early 2011 has deeply worried the ruling Al Saud family and its overriding policy focus since then has been on maintaining stability – at all costs. The Saudi authorities have ample funds. The kingdom's foreign-currency reserves have risen from just $19.8 billion in 2000 to $645 billion at the end of 2012.

The increasing urgency to create jobs, combined with the government's diminishing capacity to provide them, is one reason the government is imposing ever-stricter regulations on foreign companies to employ Saudi nationals. The kingdom's nationalisation programme is one of the more rigorous in the Gulf. Combined with a levy on companies for employing expatriate workers imposed in 2012, it is becoming increasingly costly for foreign firms.

Yet the Saudi authorities know that they must maintain the country's competitiveness if they are to generate sufficient jobs well

TABLE 2.20 **Saudi Arabia: economic indicators**

	2005	2006	2007	2008	2009	2010	2011	2012
GDP growth (% real change per year)	7.3	5.6	6.0	8.4	1.8	7.4	8.6	5.1
Nominal GDP[a] (US$bn)	328.5	376.9	416.0	519.8	429.1	526.8	669.5	711.0
Exports of goods & services (% of GDP)	57.1	59.8	59.9	62.1	47.1	49.7	56.2	56.2
Imports of goods & services (% of GDP)	24.9	30.1	34.9	34.0	37.8	33.1	29.6	30.3
Exchange rate SR:US$ (average)	3.7	3.7	3.7	3.8	3.8	3.8	3.8	3.8
Consumer price inflation (% per year, average)	0.6	2.3	4.1	9.9	5.1	5.3	3.9	2.9
Population (m)	23	24	25	26	26	27	28	29
GDP per head[b] (US$ at PPP)	21,990	23,230	24,560	26,380	26,280	27,730	29,780	30,880
Inward foreign direct investment (FDI) (US$bn)	12.1	17.1	22.8	39.5	36.5	29.2	16.3	12.4

a Real GDP (gross domestic product) is adjusted for price changes. Nominal GDP includes price effects.
b GDP per head (US$ at PPP; purchasing power parity) is calculated based on an adjustment of exchange rates to reflect differences in the cost of goods and services between countries.
Source: The Economist Intelligence Unit

into the future. This means ultimately easing regulations and other bureaucratic impositions on business and, crucially, developing the non-oil economy. Economic diversification is now a central plank of the government's development policy.

Doing business

Two issues – jobs and stability – will underpin government decision-making in the years to come. Government spending aimed at boosting household demand will favour companies that target consumers. That said, capital expenditure will also remain high over the medium term, helping companies with mainly corporate or state clients.

However, domestic demand in Saudi Arabia originates for the most part from the state and dealing with government is not easy. Understanding the decision-making process and dealing with arbitrary and opaque decisions remain central challenges for business. Many of the price and cash flow pressures stem from government as well – it increasingly demands greater value out of each contract, yet often fails to pay on time. Many companies complain that the Saudis are the worst payers in the Gulf.

In general, the most common refrain from foreign firms operating in Saudi Arabia is that it is a "complicated", "frustrating" and "awkward" place to do business. Yet, clearly, the benefits outweigh the complications. The country has all the main business growth drivers in place: a young, fast-growing population; relative wealth and rising demand; strong government spending; and a positive outlook for economic expansion.

Africa

Overview

Previously viewed as a marginal location by mainstream investors and companies, Africa is now attracting far more interest as a result of rapid economic and population growth. Real GDP growth averaged 6.4% a year in 2005–08, the best for a generation. The rebound following the global recession in 2008–09 has been swift.

Robust population growth is combining with urbanisation, increasing consumption and the emergence of a middle class to create huge opportunities. Four in ten Africans now live in cities, pushing up demand for modern goods and services, and leading to rapid growth in the information and communications technology (ICT), banking and retail sectors. Meanwhile, demand for African commodities is surging, especially from fast-growing emerging markets in Asia, led by China and India.

Perceptions of political risk have also changed – partly a result of genuine improvements. Corruption remains endemic, but a new generation of political and business leaders is acting against it. Wars, coups and revolutions have not disappeared, but they are no longer the prevalent mode of politics across the continent. For every two steps forward over the past 20 years there has been at least one step back, but the overall trend appears to be in the right direction.

Nevertheless, the business climate remains extremely challenging, especially among the larger economies (outside South Africa), and the region remains at the lower end of global doing business rankings. In particular, excessive bureaucracy and regulation continue to keep most African workers and businesses locked out of the formal economy.

Africa's growth is being spurred by a rapid increase in foreign investment. Two large oil-producing countries, Nigeria and Angola, continue to dominate inflows. But non-energy investment is growing strongly in several markets, led by South Africa, which is viewed as a gateway to sub-Saharan Africa. Companies are mainly targeting the "low-hanging" fruit – Nigeria, Ghana and Kenya, with Tanzania close behind – that represents a compromise between growth, stability and market size (or access to markets). Excitement about Ethiopia will be blunted by the costs of setting up and operating and a realistic appraisal of market size (Ethiopia's population may be large but it remains overwhelmingly poor and rural); and the infrastructural challenges in the Democratic Republic of the Congo (DRC) are monumental, even by African standards.

The sectors providing the best opportunities are ICT, banking and retail, as penetration rates for modern goods and services remain comparatively low, while significant prospects also exist in tourism, health care and manufacturing. Investment in infrastructure is also rising, driven by resources-for-investment deals by Chinese firms.

Traditional investors such as the US and western Europe remain important but have been joined by China and India. Since 2000 Chinese investment in Africa has expanded dramatically, helping to drive a boom in Sino-African trade. Meanwhile, there is increasing interest in Africa's non-oil sectors from US firms such as IBM, General Motors, Dow and Walmart, as well as European multinationals. Companies from other countries, including South Korea and Brazil, are joining the bandwagon, and South African firms are also big players in the rest of Africa.

Africa's weak infrastructure, especially power and transport, is a widespread problem, even in South Africa. Significant investment is being undertaken, but the scale of the problem defies a short-term solution. The infrastructure gap is daunting on every measure. One of the most pressing needs is investment is power – only 30% of the population have access to electricity, compared with 70–90% in the other developing regions.

Spectacular growth in mobile telephony since 2000 highlights the potential for well-structured investments in Africa's infrastructure. At that time mobile penetration rates were lower than 1% in almost every country in the region; by 2010 roughly 40% of Africans had mobile phones.

According to the UN, the population of sub-Saharan Africa is likely to double to around 2 billion people by 2040, and the demographic dividend is attracting increasing attention from investors. Some of the world's largest institutional investors intend to take their first significant step in Africa in 2013–17, according to a survey of 158 senior executives by the EIU in 2012. There are already more than 50 African cities with populations of over 1m, and several cities larger than London. The consumer market is still young and there is a large unmet demand for basic products and services.

Despite a number of obstacles and challenges, there is little doubt that Africa is now open for business, and it will be a leading priority for many multinational companies over the next ten years.

KENYA

Historical snapshot

Following independence from the UK in 1963, Kenyans were subjected to nearly 30 years of single-party rule, first under Jomo Kenyatta and later under Daniel Arap Moi. Multi-party democracy was introduced in December 1991. But until its humiliating defeat in the 2002 elections, KANU – the political party of Kenyatta and Moi – had been in power for 40 years. President Mwai Kibaki's victory in 2002 was therefore a milestone in Kenya's political history, albeit one that lost prominence with the violence that followed the 2007 elections.

Market dynamics

Politics dominates Kenyan business. However, Kenya is increasingly a middle-class society, and, with one of the region's best education systems, Kenyan voters and the local press are increasingly vocal.

The absence of mineral wealth – until recent discoveries of oil and natural gas – has made the state far more reliant on tax revenues than many other African states, and governance has improved in recent years. The Kenyan economy is, though, highly exposed to Europe: high-end tourism, which contributes 14% of GDP, is one vulnerable sector. The large market in cut flowers and fresh vegetables is another, accounting for over 10% of exports; tea accounts for another 20%.

Nairobi has long been an important hub for multilateral organisations such as the World Bank and a range of non-governmental organisations (NGOs). More recently, the city has attracted a growing number of international businesses. Although most of these use Nairobi as a hub for East Africa, some are using it as their launch pad into sub-Saharan Africa more generally, encouraged by the government's business-friendly attitude and policies, good international connections, and the city's central location and pleasant quality of life.

TABLE 2.21 **Kenya: economic indicators**

	2005	2006	2007	2008	2009	2010	2011	2012
GDP growth (% real change per year)	5.9	6.3	7.0	1.5	2.7	5.8	4.4	4.6
Nominal GDP[a] (US$bn)	18.7	22.5	27.2	30.5	30.6	32.2	34.3	40.7
Exports of goods & services (% of GDP)	27.9	27.1	26.8	27.6	24.1	27.8	28.5	27.3
Imports of goods & services (% of GDP)	37.0	37.8	37.7	41.7	37.5	40.0	45.1	44.5
Exchange rate KSh:US$ (average)	75.6	72.1	67.3	69.2	77.4	79.2	88.8	84.5
Consumer price inflation (% per year, average)	10.3	14.5	9.8	16.3	18.6	4.0	14.0	9.4
Population (m)	36	37	38	39	40	41	42	43
GDP per head[b] (US$ at PPP)	1,340	1,431	1,534	1,550	1,565	1,632	1,693	1,750
Inward foreign direct investment (FDI) (US$bn)	0.0	0.1	0.7	0.1	0.1	0.2	0.3	0.4

a Real GDP (gross domestic product) is adjusted for price changes. Nominal GDP includes price effects.
b GDP per head (US$ at PPP; purchasing power parity) is calculated based on an adjustment of exchange rates to reflect differences in the cost of goods and services between countries.
Source: The Economist Intelligence Unit

Doing business

Doing business in Kenya is certainly not without its frustrations. Traffic in Nairobi is bad: companies hoping to set up several meetings in a day, European-style, can forget it. Electricity prices are set monthly by the regulator and can be volatile, because Kenya is heavily dependent on hydroelectricity. This will change over time as geothermal power plants come on-stream. But for now, businesses, especially targeting consumers, need to be mindful of the triple shock from periods of drought: higher electricity prices; a weaker shilling as fuel imports rise and exports of agricultural products suffer; and a dent in consumer spending as a result of the weaker shilling and higher power and food costs.

There has been an increase in terrorist incidents over the past couple of years, mainly associated with Al Shabaab extremists opposed to the Somali government. The threat is something to monitor but has so far not affected middle-class suburbs in Nairobi. Violent crime is also a concern, but is nowhere near South African levels. Companies should be concerned about rising corruption, which many managers think is becoming a bigger problem in Kenya than it is in Nigeria.

Despite these obstacles, Kenya offers significant opportunities in a range of sectors. The country has a reputation for innovation, notably in telecommunications and financial services, and has attracted many IT companies to Nairobi. The advent of oil and gas, the burgeoning middle class and its prominent position in the Horn of Africa, offering access to the rest of the East African Community as well as countries like Ethiopia and South Sudan, make Kenya one of the top five destinations in Africa for business.

NIGERIA

Historical snapshot

Nigeria's modern history has been shaped by the discovery of vast oil resources in 1958. Independence from the UK was declared in 1960. Then, as now, Nigeria's future appeared promising. But the lack of a meaningful national identity combined with the oil "curse" undermined the fledgling republic. By 1967 the country had descended into civil war. Sustained democracy would not be achieved until 1999, after 33 years of military rule. Nigeria has experienced only four quasi-democratic elections, and only the most recent approached standards that could be described as free and fair.

Market dynamics

The market is still dominated by oil. It is the biggest export, and makes up 70% of government revenue. Redistribution of revenues to the poorer regions in the north, along with the relocation of the capital from Lagos in the south-west to Abuja in the middle, were designed to mitigate economic tension. That has not worked well, and the overlay of religious differences between the predominantly Muslim north and the predominantly Christian south has led to an intensification of violent incidents, notably by Boko Haram, a militant Islamist group.

Political instability and endemic corruption since independence brought about the withdrawal of most foreign interests other than oil producers. But interest has revived, owing to sustained economic growth and the spending power of more than 150m consumers. The economy is expected to outgrow South Africa's within just a few years, and that growth is coming not from oil, but from an enduring expansion in demand for middle-class goods and services. There is still plenty of scope for expansion in the telecommunications sector, particularly data services. Official statistics seriously understate the size of the Nigerian economy and the spending power of consumers.

TABLE 2.22 **Nigeria: economic indicators**

	2005	2006	2007	2008	2009	2010	2011	2012
GDP growth (% real change per year)	6.5	6.0	6.5	6.0	7.0	8.0	7.4	6.6
Nominal GDP[a] (US$bn)	112.2	145.4	166.5	208.1	169.5	229.5	245.7	262.6
Exports of goods & services (% of GDP)	31.7	43.1	33.7	39.9	30.8	39.1	52.5	50.2
Imports of goods & services (% of GDP)	19.1	21.5	30.3	25.1	31.0	29.0	36.0	37.4
Exchange rate N:US$ (average)	131.3	128.7	125.8	118.5	148.9	150.3	154.7	156.8
Consumer price inflation (% per year, average)	17.9	8.2	5.4	11.6	11.5	13.7	10.8	12.2
Population (m)	142	146	150	153	158	162	166	170
GDP per head[b] (US$ at PPP)	1,720	1,880	1,960	2,130	2,230	2,380	2,530	2,670
Inward foreign direct investment (FDI) (US$bn)	5.0	4.9	6.0	8.2	8.6	6.0	8.8	7.0

a Real GDP (gross domestic product) is adjusted for price changes. Nominal GDP includes price effects.
b GDP per head (US$ at PPP; purchasing power parity) is calculated based on an adjustment of exchange rates to reflect differences in the cost of goods and services between countries.
Source: The Economist Intelligence Unit

Doing business

Businesses operating in or considering Nigeria are quick to comment on the high levels of corruption, but veterans are adamant that it is possible to play by the rules, and indeed extremely important to do so. The current federal administration, under President Goodluck Jonathan, has put a spotlight on corruption – as has Babatunde Fashola, governor of Lagos state. In the past, international companies were able to distance themselves from certain unsavoury practices by working through agents and paying "facilitation fees". Changes in corporate governance regulations, along with reputational risk, have considerably narrowed the scope for speeding things up. As a result, companies need to be prepared for pretty much everything to take longer in Nigeria.

There is also a significant competency gap, and lower-ranking civil servants may simply be unaware of the correct procedures. Nigerian law is typically convoluted, so there are good grounds for confusion. Businesses report that it is often most effective to develop a good working relationship with the relevant minister and request clear instructions in writing that can be shown as required.

The biggest problem cited by business is the lack of a reliable power supply, which makes back-up generators, usually diesel-fuelled, mandatory. Energy reform is under way, but it is being obstructed by powerful vested interests.

International brands also complain of widespread problems with counterfeit and "grey" products. Some have come up with innovative solutions to counter this, but these add a layer of cost. Until new electronic monitoring systems are implemented at West African ports and an institutional culture of compliance created, the only real remedy is to make an enormous effort to educate consumers.

Despite the many challenges, Nigeria is a vibrant market and one that is simply too large to ignore.

SOUTH AFRICA

Historical snapshot

South Africa occupies a unique position in Africa. Its strategic location at the southernmost tip of the continent led to the birth of Cape Town back in the mid-17th century, and when vast gold deposits were discovered in the late 19th century the foundations were laid for the country to become Africa's economic powerhouse. South Africa's economic success was built on its mineral wealth, but this could not have been exploited as profitably without the vast resource of cheap manual labour. Though it is now more than 20 years since the demise of the apartheid regime in 1990, contemporary South Africa cannot be understood without taking account of the many ramifications of white minority rule.

Market dynamics

South Africa is still the continent's largest economy, but the gap is closing. Nigeria's economy, which at the beginning of the 21st century was less than half the size of South Africa's, is now only 20% smaller. With sluggish growth, serious social challenges and some restrictive legislation, businesses may well ask themselves what South Africa still has to offer.

The minerals sector is still important. Gold mining is shrinking – a reflection of ageing resources and rising operating costs – but South Africa also has vast reserves of platinum, iron and coal along with many other minerals. The capital markets are the most developed in Africa, and the banking sector is as sophisticated as any globally.

South Africa is still the easiest place to do business in Africa (after Mauritius, according to the World Bank). It is also an easy place to live, with good private schools and a stunning natural environment. But it is equally an easy place to die: violent crime casts a perpetual cloud over South African life. The private security industry is the largest in the world.

There are many less sinister opportunities. South Africa has a sizeable population of around 50m and the end of apartheid ushered in an era of unprecedented upward mobility for black South Africans. There is booming demand for middle-class goods and services.

But the economy is caught in an impasse. It is not growing quickly enough to generate the jobs needed to make a real dent in unemployment. And there is growing concern about the state's ability to implement the policies needed to ensure sustained political stability and stronger economic growth.

Doing business

During the apartheid era, many international companies pulled out of South Africa. So the economy became rather insular, and competition in many sectors was limited. The situation is changing as new international players penetrate the market, bringing greater economies of scale thanks to global supply chains – Walmart being an example. Margins will eventually come down, but in the meantime there is plenty of hay to be made, particularly in the retail sector.

In the telecommunications sector, the uptake of new technology has been slowed by the dominance of Telkom, a South African parastatal telecommunications provider. Business models that have been extraordinarily successful elsewhere, such as those leveraging the cost-effectiveness of VoIP (voice over internet protocol) technology, are still fairly new in South Africa.

Labour laws in South Africa are extremely rigid and productivity is low, despite spiralling payroll costs (double-digit annual wage increases are common). It is difficult and expensive to lay off permanent members of staff, but fixed-term contracts for tasks of a permanent nature are prohibited. To get around this, firms have historically used "labour brokers", but legislative changes are now targeting this practice. Companies must be careful to comply with hiring rules as well, notably black empowerment laws.

Nevertheless, by comparison with many OECD countries, working conditions are favourable to employers: working hours are relatively long; statutory annual leave is short; there are no mandatory contributions to workers' pension funds; and health and safety regulations are far more lax.

Even though the labour laws are highly protective of workers, industrial action is increasing, and is becoming more violent. With youth unemployment estimated at 60%, and deepening income inequality, there is a serious risk that simmering social unrest will boil over in the medium term.

South Africa's economic weight will guarantee it attention for several years, but the increasing cost and risk of doing business there give rise to serious questions about its medium-term prospects.

TABLE 2.23 **South Africa: economic indicators**

	2005	2006	2007	2008	2009	2010	2011	2012
GDP growth (% real change per year)	5.3	5.6	5.5	3.6	−1.5	3.1	3.5	2.5
Nominal GDP[a] (US$bn)	247.0	261.3	286.1	273.2	285.7	363.5	401.9	384.6
Exports of goods & services (% of GDP)	27.4	30.0	31.5	35.9	27.3	27.4	29.3	28.3
Imports of goods & services (% of GDP)	27.9	32.5	34.2	38.9	28.2	27.6	29.9	31.3
Exchange rate R:US$ (average)	6.4	6.8	7.0	8.3	8.4	7.3	7.3	8.2
Consumer price inflation (% per year, average)	2.1	3.2	6.2	10.1	7.2	4.1	5.0	5.7
Population (m)	48	49	50	50	51	52	52	52
GDP per head[b] (US$ at PPP)	8,412	9,040	9,682	10,119	9,931	10,257	10,731	11,109
Inward foreign direct investment (FDI) (US$bn)	6.5	−0.2	5.7	9.6	5.4	1.2	5.9	4.6

a Real GDP (gross domestic product) is adjusted for price changes. Nominal GDP includes price effects.
b GDP per head (US$ at PPP; purchasing power parity) is calculated based on an adjustment of exchange rates to reflect differences in the cost of goods and services between countries.
Source: The Economist Intelligence Unit

Latin America

Overview

Latin America has been attracting record levels of foreign direct investment (FDI) in recent years. There are certainly good reasons to invest. The environment for business is better than ever; democracy has taken root; and the economy is growing strongly, fuelled by a consumer-spending boom and the development of the region's abundant natural resources.

The region attracted a record $153.5 billion of FDI in 2011, with the two largest markets, Brazil and Mexico, accounting for 43.6% and 12.6% respectively of the total. The investment level is even catching up with that of China.

Much of the interest is concentrated in the natural resources sectors, fuelled by high global commodity prices. But business interest is much broader and becoming more sophisticated. Mexico is now a top choice for manufacturing, especially of low-cost components, while Brazil is the favourite for European multinationals setting up new R&D centres – and this in turn is helping to spread technical expertise more widely in the economy.

The success of government in reducing poverty and inequality has helped too. Along with better access to credit, it has allowed a new middle class to blossom, which means a huge market for consumer goods. The EIU expects the region as a whole to grow by just below 4% annually to 2017.

However, there is a long list of problems, including weak competition, rigid labour markets, rickety infrastructure and a lack of people with the skills for working in a modern economy.

Improving the situation is far from straightforward. Reforms are unpopular among large sections of voters. And even if governments wanted to push through unpopular policies, many ruling parties in the region lack the parliamentary majority to do so or are based on wobbly coalitions. In Mexico, for example, President Enrique Peña Nieto is having to negotiate opposition support to get his policies adopted, such as opening the energy sector to private investment. Moreover, there is little room in national budgets for long-term but essential investment in education and infrastructure, following the major spending programmes adopted in the aftermath of the 2008 global economic crisis. Nor is the private sector ready to step in.

Drug-related crime is widespread and social turbulence is growing because of frustration about the slow pace of change and continued inequality. Brazil experienced a spate of large-scale protests in 2013. There has been social unrest over mining projects in the Andes. And Mexico, Central America and the Caribbean have experienced violence, with Honduras, El Salvador and Jamaica suffering the highest homicide rates in the world. Drug-related organised crime also corrupts the effectiveness of government on which foreign investors depend.

Latin America will remain an attractive region for business, but questions remain over whether it can realise its potential.

ARGENTINA

Historical snapshot

Argentina has continued to suffer from a tendency to economic "boom and bust" since returning to democracy in 1983. Economic liberalisation led to remarkable growth in the 1990s, but that was followed by default in 2001. Néstor Kirchner oversaw a robust economic recovery after his election in 2003. But his wife, Cristina Fernández de Kirchner, who succeeded him in 2007, has presided over a hard landing, because of poor economic policymaking and increasing state interference in key sectors.

Market dynamics

Despite the deteriorating business environment and volatile economy, Argentina is still of interest to investors, mainly because of abundant natural resources. The country has significant oil and gas deposits, and the recently discovered Vaca Muerta shale formation is probably the third largest in the world, after those in the US and China. Argentina also has vast expanses of arable land; agriculture has been booming in recent years thanks to high prices, particularly for soyabeans, the main agricultural export.

Its population of around 40m is the fourth largest in Latin America and is relatively young and affluent: GDP per head is among the highest in the region (although inequality is also high). The labour force is relatively well-educated, productive and flexible.

Access to Mercosur, the Southern Cone customs union, is another big advantage, especially given Argentina's proximity to Brazil. Booming demand from its neighbour has been an important driver for Argentina's manufacturing sector, especially the automotive industry. One worry is that high inflation and wage growth are eroding competitiveness.

Doing business

It is becoming increasingly difficult to do business in Argentina. President Kirchner has pursued increasingly ad-hoc and unpredictable

TABLE 2.24 **Argentina: economic indicators**

	2005	2006	2007	2008	2009	2010	2011	2012
GDP growth (% real change per year)	9.2	8.5	8.7	6.8	0.9	9.2	8.9	1.9
Nominal GDP[a] (US$bn)	183.2	214.3	262.5	328.5	308.7	370.3	448.2	477.0
Exports of goods & services (% of GDP)	25.1	24.8	24.6	24.5	21.4	21.7	21.8	19.7
Imports of goods & services (% of GDP)	19.2	19.2	20.3	20.7	16.0	18.4	19.5	17.4
Exchange rate Ps:US$ (average)	2.9	3.1	3.1	3.1	3.7	3.9	4.1	4.5
Consumer price inflation (% per year, average)	9.6	10.9	8.8	12.4	17.2	22.9	24.4	25.3
Population (m)	39	39	39	40	40	41	41	41
GDP per head[b] (US$ at PPP)	10,872	12,051	13,340	14,410	14,530	15,910	17,520	18,010
Inward foreign direct investment (FDI) (US$bn)	5.3	5.5	6.5	9.7	4.0	7.8	9.9	12.6

a Real GDP (gross domestic product) is adjusted for price changes. Nominal GDP includes price effects.
b GDP per head (US$ at PPP; purchasing power parity) is calculated based on an adjustment of exchange rates to reflect differences in the cost of goods and services between countries.
Source: The Economist Intelligence Unit

interventionist policies. Spanish-owned Repsol-YPF, the country's largest oil company, was nationalised in 2012, and Argentina has a poor track record on international dispute settlement. Prospects for the energy sector are not promising: there are long-standing tariff freezes and a lack of financing to develop new projects. But even though contract rights are being eroded, a wave of nationalisations remains unlikely.

Another problem is a growing number of protectionist measures, including comprehensive trade, foreign-exchange and capital controls, introduced to limit the deterioration of the balance of payments. Although in theory it welcomes FDI, the government favours domestic investment, and a law passed in early 2012 limits foreign land ownership, which will make it tougher for foreign investors to get into the agricultural sector. Competition policy is weak – Argentina has a tradition of crony capitalism – and the tax system is cumbersome.

It is not all grim, though. President Kirchner's second term ends in 2015, and a more market-friendly government is possible after that. Companies that stay the course could then reap the rewards of the country's vast potential. A return to 1990s-style liberalisation is unlikely, however, as the privatisations carried out then are blamed for the 2001 default and subsequent crisis.

CHILE

Historical snapshot

Chile has been a pioneer in Latin America in constructing a successful open and liberal economy, and has the region's highest standard of living. It has enjoyed uninterrupted political stability since the end of the Pinochet dictatorship in 1990 and strong political consensus. This has allowed rapid economic growth (averaging 6% annually since 1990), enabling the country to escape the 2008–09 global crisis – as well as a devastating earthquake in 2010 – relatively unscathed.

Market dynamics

Chile is the smallest of Latin America's "big seven" economies. But the middle class is relatively affluent. The Chilean government and bureaucracy have long been recognised for their professionalism and low levels of corruption even by developed-country standards. There is legal certainty and a strong respect for property rights. Crime is among the lowest in Latin America.

Because of the country's small population (barely 17m), manufacturing is modest, and Chile imports many of its consumer durables – for example, it is the only country among the "big seven" not to assemble motor vehicles. But a vibrant and competitive domestic economy has allowed Chilean companies to position themselves as regional leaders, mainly in service industries such as retail. Local and foreign firms compete on an equal footing, which has made Chile a stepping-stone for companies looking to establish themselves in the region.

Along with Mexico, Chile has the region's largest network of free-trade agreements, including with the US, the EU, Japan and China. But around half of trade consists of mining, of which copper forms the bulk (40% of all exports). As China accounts for the largest share of copper demand, there is now strong synchronisation with China's economic cycle; Chile is vulnerable whenever the Asian giant slows down.

Energy is both a challenge and an opportunity. Chile suffers from some of the highest energy costs in the region, as it has to import

TABLE 2.25 **Chile: economic indicators**

	2005	2006	2007	2008	2009	2010	2011	2012
GDP growth (% real change per year)	6.2	5.7	5.2	3.3	−1.0	5.8	5.9	5.6
Nominal GDP[a] (US$bn)	123.1	154.7	173.1	179.6	172.3	217.6	251.2	268.3
Exports of goods & services (% of GDP)	40.3	43.9	45.2	41.5	37.2	38.1	38.0	34.2
Imports of goods & services (% of GDP)	31.8	29.6	31.9	39.5	29.6	31.8	34.7	33.9
Exchange rate Ps:US$ (average)	559.8	530.3	522.5	522.5	559.6	510.2	483.7	486.5
Consumer price inflation (% per year, average)	3.1	3.4	4.4	8.7	1.5	1.4	3.3	3.0
Population (m)	16	16	17	17	17	17	17	17
GDP per head[b] (US$ at PPP)	12,705	13,719	14,698	15,363	15,190	16,120	17,260	18,390
Inward foreign direct investment (FDI) (US$bn)	7.1	7.4	12.6	15.5	12.9	15.4	22.9	30.3

a Real GDP (gross domestic product) is adjusted for price changes. Nominal GDP includes price effects.
b GDP per head (US$ at PPP; purchasing power parity) is calculated based on an adjustment of exchange rates to reflect differences in the cost of goods and services between countries.
Source: The Economist Intelligence Unit

most of its oil and gas. There is large potential for clean energy such as solar and geothermal, but investment thus far has been low. Nevertheless, energy investments are a government priority, and are likely to increase. There is also a push to promote high-value-added industries and exploit Chile's potential in areas such as agro-industry, construction and forestry.

Doing business

Chile has one of the most attractive business environments in Latin America. The domestic economy is highly dynamic and foreign firms are usually able to find a niche, although competition is often fierce. Chile also boasts a large and sophisticated financial sector, by far the biggest in the region relative to the country's size (credit exceeds 80% of GDP).

On the downside, student unrest in 2011 highlighted the need to address structural shortcomings, many of them a legacy of the Pinochet era. Chief among these is education, which has underperformed despite being mostly privately funded. Skill shortages have led to programmes such as Startup Chile, which seek to attract high-tech talent from abroad. The labour market is seen by businesses as too rigid.

A key question will be how far Chile's politics can return to the tradition of consensus seen during 1990–2010. Increased discord will not preclude continued high rates of growth and improving standards of living, but it could delay the medium-term objective of making Chile the first Latin American country to achieve first-world status.

COLOMBIA

Historical snapshot

Over the past 15 years there has been a sharp reversal of fortunes for Colombia – from a country plagued by guerrillas and drug-traffickers and a greatly debilitated state to one of Latin America's most attractive countries for business. But it still faces challenges, most importantly finding a long-term solution to its 50-year-old civil conflict.

Market dynamics

Security gains have allowed investment to flow to previously conflict-infested areas. Colombia's institutions are relatively strong, and economic management has been prudent. From 2000 to 2011 the economy expanded by an annual average of 4.2%, compared with 3.3% for Latin America as a whole. The country also proved resilient during the 2008–09 global crisis.

The government has improved the business environment by reducing administrative hurdles, strengthening investor protection and creating a network of free-trade agreements, including with the US (its main trading and investment partner), the EU and non-traditional trading partners (particularly in Asia). On the policy side, there is little risk. Colombia's institutions are fiercely independent, including the judicial system and central bank, and the government is bound by new budget rules. A return to investment-grade status for the country's sovereign debt has been an additional bonus.

Colombia is the third most populous country in Latin America and its young population is expected to reach almost 51m by 2016, compared with 46m in 2011. At the same time, continued urbanisation, falling poverty levels and rising household incomes make for a growing consumer market.

The country also benefits from a wealth of natural resources. Since the early 1990s there have been large discoveries of oil and mineral resources, and changes in regulation have encouraged private-sector involvement and led to higher production. Colombia is now a significant oil producer, with output expected to reach 1m barrels a day in 2014.

TABLE 2.26 **Colombia: economic indicators**

	2005	2006	2007	2008	2009	2010	2011	2012
GDP growth (% real change per year)	4.7	6.7	6.9	3.5	1.7	4.0	6.6	4.0
Nominal GDP[a] (US$bn)	146.6	162.8	207.5	244.3	233.9	287.0	336.4	369.6
Exports of goods & services (% of GDP)	16.9	17.6	16.5	17.8	16.0	15.9	18.9	18.3
Imports of goods & services (% of GDP)	18.8	20.5	19.8	20.3	18.2	17.8	19.8	19.7
Exchange rate Ps:US$ (average)	2,321.1	2,358.6	2,077.8	1,965.1	2,157.6	1,899.0	1,848.0	1,798.0
Consumer price inflation (% per year, average)	5.1	4.3	5.5	7.0	4.2	2.3	3.4	3.2
Population (m)	44	45	45	46	46	47	48	48
GDP per head[b] (US$ at PPP)	7,180	7,789	8,444	8,809	8,910	9,260	9,950	10,390
Inward foreign direct investment (FDI) (US$bn)	10.3	6.7	9.5	10.2	7.1	6.8	13.4	15.8

a Real GDP (gross domestic product) is adjusted for price changes. Nominal GDP includes price effects.
b GDP per head (US$ at PPP; purchasing power parity) is calculated based on an adjustment of exchange rates to reflect differences in the cost of goods and services between countries.
Source: The Economist Intelligence Unit

This has led to concerns that the economy may suffer from so-called "Dutch disease" – an overreliance on natural resources to the detriment of other sectors – with steady appreciation of the peso in the past few years. This has hurt competitiveness in non-energy sectors, including manufacturing and agriculture, two large sources of employment. According to local surveys, the strength of the peso is the private sector's biggest concern.

Doing business

A big hindrance is Colombia's poor infrastructure, which is lagging behind the expansion of the economy. There are road and port bottlenecks, and air and rail facilities are inadequate. This is partly because of the state's poor implementation capacity. Progress on efforts to streamline procedures has been slow, especially at the local and regional level. Corruption is prevalent, especially in public tenders.

The poverty ratio is still over 30%, and income and regional inequalities are among the highest in the world. Educational levels are extremely low, contributing to one of the highest unemployment levels among Latin America's large economies.

Internal conflict has also impaired development. The left-wing guerrillas (the FARC and ELN) have been weakened, and a large part of the right-wing paramilitary groups demobilised, but the conflict carries on. It is clear that the military solution pursued so far has been inadequate, and that a political solution is needed. But reaching a long-lasting agreement has proved complex.

Looking back at what has been achieved in recent years, however, makes it difficult not to foresee an auspicious future for Colombia.

MEXICO

Historical snapshot

Mexico was among the first economies in Latin America to liberalise during the 1980s and 1990s, capping this with the North American Free Trade Agreement (NAFTA) in 1994 with the US and Canada. But it has not been smooth sailing since then. The country suffered a devastating financial crisis in 1994/95, and more recently the steepest recession in the western hemisphere during the 2009 global crisis. Despite this, Mexico has emerged as one of Latin America's most dynamic economies in the past few years, outgrowing Brazil in both 2011 and 2012.

Market dynamics

Mexico is the second largest economy in Latin America and one of the few "trillion-dollar" economies in the world. Per-head income is high by regional standards (around 25% higher than Brazil's in purchasing-power parity terms), although this masks high inequality.

The economy rests on a dynamic export-based manufacturing sector – mostly foreign multinationals, but an increasing number of Mexican firms too. These companies have taken advantage of proximity to the US market and relatively low labour costs – now estimated to be just 20% higher than China's (compared with three times higher at the beginning of the 21st century). All the "big three" US carmakers have production facilities in Mexico, as do many of their European and Japanese counterparts. Mexico is also an important producer of electronic equipment, white goods and other consumer durables, and textiles.

Unfortunately, the domestic economy shares little of this dynamism. Most non-import/export sectors are dominated by a monopoly or cartel of Mexican firms. These have used their local profits to expand abroad, to Latin America and, increasingly, the US. Telmex/América Móvil epitomises this: it has used its stranglehold on the Mexican market to turn itself into Latin America's largest telecoms firm. The same situation can be seen in the media, cement and food processing sectors, among others.

TABLE 2.27 **Mexico: economic indicators**

	2005	2006	2007	2008	2009	2010	2011	2012
GDP growth (% real change per year)	3.2	5.1	3.2	1.2	−6.0	5.3	3.9	3.9
Nominal GDP[a] (US$bn)	848.6	951.7	1,035.0	1,093.8	882.9	1,034.2	1,158.4	1,177.2
Exports of goods & services (% of GDP)	27.1	28.0	28.0	28.1	27.6	30.3	31.6	32.9
Imports of goods & services (% of GDP)	28.6	29.2	29.5	30.3	29.1	31.6	32.8	34.0
Exchange rate Ps:US$ (average)	10.9	10.9	10.9	11.1	13.5	12.6	12.4	13.2
Consumer price inflation (% per year, average)	4.0	3.6	4.0	5.1	5.3	4.2	3.4	4.1
Population (m)	106	108	109	110	111	113	114	115
GDP per head[b] (US$ at PPP)	12,218	13,545	14,601	15,534	15,053	16,304	17,093	17,906
Inward foreign direct investment (FDI) (US$bn)	24.4	20.3	31.4	27.9	16.6	21.4	21.5	12.7

a Real GDP (gross domestic product) is adjusted for price changes. Nominal GDP includes price effects.
b GDP per head (US$ at PPP; purchasing power parity) is calculated based on an adjustment of exchange rates to reflect differences in the cost of goods and services between countries.
Source: The Economist Intelligence Unit

One of the most potentially lucrative sectors, energy, is still state-owned, but private investment will probably be allowed in the next few years to take advantage of the discovery of deep-water oil in the Gulf of Mexico and exploit the country's large shale gas reserves.

Doing business

Mexico is attractive for multinational firms seeking to gain a foothold in the US market or in Latin America. Infrastructure is generally good by regional standards. The manufacturing sector is increasingly sophisticated – for instance, an aerospace industry has emerged. A persistently weak peso since 2010 has also been a boon for exporting firms, although not for domestic consumers.

On the downside, there is a persistent war between drug-traffickers in certain regions (notably along the US border and in some Pacific states), although large firms have mostly been spared and foreigners are seldom directly targeted. Corruption is rife. There are skill shortages, and labour relations can be difficult – although unionisation is weak in the export sector.

Despite the end of 70 years of single-party rule in 2000, democracy has failed to dislodge interest groups such as unions and big domestic businesses. The banking sector has become more resilient, however, and monetary and macroeconomic policies have improved. But Mexico needs a more energised challenge to entrenched interests to realise its full potential. The Partido Revolucionario Institucional (PRI) government has put reform at the top of its agenda. But it has historic links to many of these interests, so success may be mixed.

PERU

Historical snapshot

Since the beginning of the 21st century Peru has shifted from being mainly associated with a long, bloody campaign of political violence by Maoist guerrillas, the Shining Path, to being one of the fastest-growing economies in Latin America. Reforms during the 1990s under Alberto Fujimori (currently serving a 25-year jail sentence for human-rights violations and corruption) encouraged investment and laid the foundations for rapid growth. And the arrest of the Shining Path leadership has led to improved security.

Market dynamics

Peru has a population of 30m, a large proportion of which (around 8.5m) lives in the capital, Lima. GDP per head (at purchasing-power parity) lags behind that of Mexico and Chile but is close to neighbouring Colombia and only just behind Brazil. It has almost doubled over the past ten years and should continue to rise rapidly to 2020. The rapidly expanding middle class is fuelling a consumption boom.

Strong global demand and high prices for Peru's metal exports – the mainstay of the economy – have supported growth and boosted domestic business confidence. This led to strong expansion of private investment and consumption, the main drivers of growth since 2009. The economy is currently well-balanced.

Fears that President Ollanta Humala, elected in early 2011, would veer away from an orthodox and pragmatic policy mix have largely dissipated. He had adopted a radical leftist platform in previous campaigns, but he moderated his stance for the 2011 vote, and surprised critics by filling his cabinet with centrist technocrats.

Peru has a wealth of mineral deposits, particularly copper, gold and zinc. Oil has been found in the Amazon and in other eastern river basins, and offshore in the north. Huge natural-gas deposits, notably Camisea, in the central and southern forests have been developed in recent years. Peru has mining projects worth over $50 billion in the pipeline.

TABLE 2.28 **Peru: economic indicators**

	2005	2006	2007	2008	2009	2010	2011	2012
GDP growth (% real change per year)	6.8	7.7	8.9	9.8	0.9	8.8	6.9	6.3
Nominal GDP[a] (US$bn)	79.4	92.3	107.3	126.9	127.0	153.8	176.6	199.4
Exports of goods & services (% of GDP)	25.1	28.5	29.1	27.3	24.0	25.5	28.7	25.5
Imports of goods & services (% of GDP)	19.2	19.9	22.4	27.1	20.4	22.8	24.8	24.5
Exchange rate Ns:US$ (average)	3.3	3.3	3.1	2.9	3.0	2.8	2.8	2.6
Consumer price inflation (% per year, average)	1.6	2.0	1.8	5.8	2.9	1.5	3.4	3.7
Population (m)	28	28	29	29	30	30	30	31
GDP per head[b] (US$ at PPP)	6,306	6,912	7,638	8,453	8,490	9,220	9,930	10,600
Inward foreign direct investment (FDI) (US$bn)	2.6	3.5	5.5	6.9	6.4	8.5	8.2	12.3

a Real GDP (gross domestic product) is adjusted for price changes. Nominal GDP includes price effects.
b GDP per head (US$ at PPP; purchasing power parity) is calculated based on an adjustment of exchange rates to reflect differences in the cost of goods and services between countries.
Source: The Economist Intelligence Unit

Doing business

However, the rapid development of large-scale mining has exposed one of the major risks to Peru's broadly positive outlook: social conflict. Demonstrations over environmental and other social issues have become a regular problem. These conflicts, often violent, have exposed the deep urban/rural divide in the country. Rural communities feel that they have yet to benefit from Peru's rapid development this century. The gap in income levels and access to services between rural and urban communities remains wide.

Other weaknesses in Peru's business environment include substandard institutions, underdeveloped infrastructure, rigidities in the labour market and a tax code that needs reform. Public investment in infrastructure, and a push to develop more comprehensive social programmes, will go some way towards helping to integrate the market, but the potential for social unrest will remain high.

Nevertheless, pro-business policies are likely to persist, as market reforms – including dispute settlement and intellectual property enforcement – have been locked in by numerous free-trade agreements. The country also offers huge scope for growth in consumer expenditure. Improving access to credit, strong forecast growth and resilience to external shocks (the economy grew by 0.9% during the 2009 downturn) mean that Peru is likely to continue to hold an important place in companies' Latin America strategies.

VENEZUELA

Historical snapshot

Thirty years ago Venezuela was one of Latin America's most vigorous democracies and wealthiest countries, but a period of decay, marked by corruption and demagoguery, led to rising poverty and inequality. Under Hugo Chávez's populist rule there was a renewed interest in social policies but also social polarisation, a weakening of the country's institutions and rising economic distortions. The president died in March 2013, but it appears that "chavismo" will remain in power for the time being.

Market dynamics

Venezuela has vast reserves of natural resources, including gas, coal and precious metals, an array of spectacular natural tourist attractions and a relatively good physical infrastructure. It enjoys important demographic advantages, including a young population. Venezuelans are avid consumers, as well as being health- and image-conscious.

And then there is oil. The petroleum industry has dominated the economy since oil extraction gained momentum after the first world war, and Venezuela has been a major producer ever since. Although output is below its 1998 peak, the country boasts what it claims are the world's largest oil reserves, at close to 300 billion barrels, meaning that it could sustain current production for another hundred years.

Despite the promises of various administrations (including the current one) to diversify the economy, Venezuela is plagued by "Dutch disease", with oil accounting for over 95% of total foreign earnings. There has also been little progress in putting systems in place to mitigate oil-price volatility. Chávez's policies exacerbated the situation, and the economy has grown only modestly in the past few years despite massive fiscal spending.

Doing business

Venezuela has the most challenging business environment of Latin America's major economies. Although it remains an attractive market, day-to-day operations are complicated by the region's highest

TABLE 2.29 **Venezuela: economic indicators**

	2005	2006	2007	2008	2009	2010	2011	2012
GDP growth (% real change per year)	10.3	9.9	8.8	5.3	−3.2	−1.5	4.2	5.6
Nominal GDP[a] (US$bn)	145.5	183.5	230.4	315.6	329.4	392.0	316.5	382.5
Exports of goods & services (% of GDP)	39.7	36.5	31.1	30.8	18.1	28.5	29.9	25.8
Imports of goods & services (% of GDP)	20.5	22.1	25.1	21.0	20.4	17.6	19.7	22.9
Exchange rate BsF:US$ (average)	2.1	2.1	2.1	2.1	2.1	2.6	4.3	4.3
Consumer price inflation (% per year, average)	16.0	13.7	18.7	30.4	27.1	28.2	26.1	21.1
Population (m)	27	27	27	28	28	29	29	30
GDP per head[b] (US$ at PPP)	9,970	11,160	12,280	13,000	12,500	12,270	12,860	13,620
Inward foreign direct investment (FDI) (US$bn)	2.7	0.2	2.5	1.3	−2.6	1.9	3.9	2.2

a Real GDP (gross domestic product) is adjusted for price changes. Nominal GDP includes price effects.
b GDP per head (US$ at PPP; purchasing power parity) is calculated based on an adjustment of exchange rates to reflect differences in the cost of goods and services between countries.
Source: The Economist Intelligence Unit

inflation rate, strict price and exchange controls, some of the world's most restrictive labour laws, a complicated tax regime, widespread corruption and considerable bureaucratic costs.

Attitudes towards private enterprise, competition and foreign investment have swung wildly. The present government is pursuing a statist economic approach, and although it remains open to private investment in certain areas (including oil), it has a strong ideological opposition to market competition. Administrative capacity has dwindled as the government systemically rewards political loyalty over technical competence. But perhaps the main hindrance has been the erosion of the legal framework for investors and continual threats of nationalisations.

Following Chávez's death, a chavista candidate, Nicolás Maduro, was elected president. Under chavismo there will be some room for pragmatic policies – the oil sector requires significant investment and technology from foreign partners – but Venezuela will continue to lag behind as an investment destination, and economic volatility will hinder catch-up with wealthier countries.

Index

PublicAffairs is a publishing house founded in 1997. It is a tribute to the standards, values, and flair of three persons who have served as mentors to countless reporters, writers, editors, and book people of all kinds, including me.

I. F. STONE, proprietor of *I. F. Stone's Weekly*, combined a commitment to the First Amendment with entrepreneurial zeal and reporting skill and became one of the great independent journalists in American history. At the age of eighty, Izzy published *The Trial of Socrates*, which was a national bestseller. He wrote the book after he taught himself ancient Greek.

BENJAMIN C. BRADLEE was for nearly thirty years the charismatic editorial leader of *The Washington Post*. It was Ben who gave the *Post* the range and courage to pursue such historic issues as Watergate. He supported his reporters with a tenacity that made them fearless and it is no accident that so many became authors of influential, best-selling books.

ROBERT L. BERNSTEIN, the chief executive of Random House for more than a quarter century, guided one of the nation's premier publishing houses. Bob was personally responsible for many books of political dissent and argument that challenged tyranny around the globe. He is also the founder and longtime chair of Human Rights Watch, one of the most respected human rights organizations in the world.

•   •   •

For fifty years, the banner of Public Affairs Press was carried by its owner Morris B. Schnapper, who published Gandhi, Nasser, Toynbee, Truman, and about 1,500 other authors. In 1983, Schnapper was described by *The Washington Post* as "a redoubtable gadfly." His legacy will endure in the books to come.

Peter Osnos, *Founder and Editor-at-Large*